Luke;

What He Said...

Brendan Cullen

Revised and Updated May 2020

LUKE; What he said…

Copyright © 2020 by Brendan Cullen

ISBN: 9798616623218

Cover design by Brendan Cullen

Copyright © 2020 by Brendan Cullen

Cover Art by Srdjan Filipovic

Cover Design contributor: Ashley Mak

For bulk order discounts, email brendanpcullen@gmail.com

Paperback and Kindle also available from Amazon.com

Used by permission

RSV Revised Standard Version

KJV King James Version

ASV American Standard Version

ESV "Scripture quotations are from the ESV® Bible (The Holy Bible, English Standard Version®), copyright © 2001 by Crossway, a publishing ministry of Good News Publishers. Used by permission. All rights reserved."

NKJV" Scripture taken from the New King James Version®. Copyright © 1982 by Thomas Nelson. Used by permission. All rights reserved.

Scripture quotations taken from the New American Standard Bible® (NASB),

Copyright © 1960, 1962, 1963, 1968, 1971, 1972, 1973,

1975, 1977, 1995 by The Lockman Foundation

Used by permission. www.Lockman.org"

"Scripture quotations taken from the Amplified® Bible (AMP),

Copyright © 2015 by The Lockman Foundation

Used by permission. www.Lockman.org"

CJB Taken from the Complete Jewish Bible by David H. Stern. Copyright © 1998. All rights reserved. Used by permission of Messianic Jewish Publishers, 6120 Day Long Lane, Clarksville, MD 21029. www.messianicjewish.net.

Scriptures taken from the Holy Bible, New International Version®, NIV®. Copyright © 1973, 1978, 1984, 2011 by Biblica, Inc.™ Used by permission of Zondervan. All rights reserved worldwide. www.zondervan.com The "NIV" and "New International Version" are trademarks registered in the United States Patent and Trademark Office by Biblica,

Scripture quotations taken from the New American Standard Bible® (NASB), Copyright © 1960, 1962, 1963, 1968, 1971, 1972, 1973, 1975, 1977, 1995 by The Lockman Foundation Used by permission. www.Lockman.org

LUKE; What He Said...

DEDICATION

For my wife Cindy, my love, who has stood with me through everything.

"He who finds a wife finds a good thing
And obtains favor from the LORD." **Proverbs 18:22 NASB**

Special thanks to the following people for their encouragement and input.

Avi Ron, Pat Stayton, Jim Veihl, Desi Cullen,   Michael Desgrosselliers.

The Setting

This narrative is based on the Book of Luke which is set in the first century CE of what is considered modern history. Modern history uses the approximate birth of Jesus Christ as the refence point.

The Roman empire had conquered most of the known world and ruled it with violence and oppression. Subjects had few civil rights, amputation and/or death was often the punishment for minor crimes. Slavery was the norm for non-Roman citizens.

The narrative takes place in the region of modern-day Israel and Palestine. The culture was Hebraic, in other words many were descended from the tribes of Moses and Abraham. They believed in the God of Abraham, Isaac and Jacob. His name is YAWEH. The people understood from prophecies that God would send a deliverer, a savior, a Messiah to set them free. The people anxiously awaited His arrival. They had not heard anything from God's prophets for about 400+ years. God had been silent. This was until John the Baptist arrived on the scene proclaiming the arrival of the Messiah. Most thought that the Messiah would deliver them from Roman rule and oppression. What he actually came to do was to free them from their sins and punishment.

Jesus (Yeshua) was from the lineage of Abraham and was 100% Jewish. A Jewish Messiah for a Jewish people. As part of the new covenant established by Jesus, non-Jews that accepted Jesus as the Messiah were included in this new covenant of Repentance and Salvation.

LUKE; What He Said...

Table of contents

Authors Note:

When I became curious about Christianity, it had been suggested to me that I read the book of John; then decide for myself. I agreed to give it a try. Boy was that a mistake! "In the beginning was the Word and the Word was with God and the Word was God". What??? I was immediately thinking there was no possible way I could understand this book; I put it down for many years.

As a new Christian I found that the bible was very difficult reading, intimidating and foreign to me. The strange name of books, so many chapters and verses and to top it off, a bunch of terms and words I had never heard of before. It seemed to be written for someone with a better education and intellect than I had.

After reading more than twenty versions, some many times; I realized that there was so much I didn't understand correctly. I thought that if I had trouble, there was a good chance that others did also. I decided it might be good to have a short and easy to understand introduction to the bible that would encourage reading the Bible, and what better way than an easy to read story.

This document is not to be considered Scripture and is not intended to be used for study or doctrine.

I hope you enjoy this as your journey may begin today.

brendanpcullen@gmail.com

LUKE; What He Said...

1

The birth of John the Baptizer and conception of Jesus

There have been many stories circulating around about a man Named Jesus. With all the variations, I decided to write an accurate narrative based on countless interviews with eye witnesses, including family members who were witness to the life of this man. It is truly astonishing.

Around the time in history, early in the first century CE. In other words when history went from BC to AD. Jesus lived mostly in the area of modern-day Israel in the Middle East. Herod was King over area of Judah. Around this time here was a priest who served in the temple by the name of Zechariah who was married to a woman named Elizabeth. They were very good, kind and generous people. They followed the teachings of the Jewish faith closely. They didn't not have any children.

Now the priests took turns attending to the temple duties. Zechariah went into the temple to burn incense while everyone else were outside praying. While he was in there an angel sent from God appeared to him. The angel told him not to be afraid and that his prayer had been heard. You wife is going to give birth to a baby boy. He will bring great joy to you. You will be delighted with him. Many people are going to be excited when he is born. God will consider him great.

I have instructions for you. He is never to drink liquor or wine. He will be filled with the Holy Spirit from his mother's womb. He will be a great preacher. He will turn many of the people of Israel to THE LORD their God. He will go on before the Lord, in the spirit and power of Elijah, to turn the hearts of the parents to their children and the disobedient to the wisdom of the righteous--to make ready a people prepared for the Lord. (Malachi 4:6)

Zechariah replied "My wife and I are too old, how is this possible?" "I am Gabriel and I stand in the presence of God. I was sent to give you this good news. But, because you didn't believe me, you will be mute, unable to speak until the child is born."

Meanwhile, the people that were waiting for Zechariah were wondering what was taking him so long. But when he came out unable to talk to them, they realized that he had seen a vision in the Temple; unable to talk, he had to communicate to them with signs.

When the time of his Temple service was over, he returned home. Following this, Elizabeth his wife conceived, and she stayed five months in seclusion, saying, "THE LORD has done this for me; he has shown me great favor and removed my public shame."

When Elizabeth was six months along, the angel Gabriel was sent by God to a city in Galilee called Nazareth, to a girl who was engaged[1] to a man named Joseph. He had descended from the great King David. Her name was Mary. Approaching her, the angel said, "Great and complete peace on you, favored young lady! THE LORD is with you!" She wondered and thought what a strange greeting this was and what it means. The angel said to her, "Don't be afraid Mary, you have found favor with God. You will become pregnant, you will give birth to a son, and you are to name him Jesus.[2] He will be great; he will be called Son of The Most High. THE LORD, God, will give him the throne of his forefather David; and he will rule the House of Jacob forever and there will be no end to his Kingdom." "How is this possible?" asked Mary since I'm a virgin?" The angel replied,

"The Holy Spirit of God will come over you, the power of The Most High will cover you. You will give birth to a boy who will be called the Son of God."

The angel then told her "You have a relative whose name is Elizabeth. She is old and has not had any children. But she has conceived a son and is six months pregnant; Because with God, nothing is impossible." Mary answered the angel "I am the servant of THE LORD; may it happen to me as you have said." Then the angel left her.

Right away, Mary headed to the town in the hill country of Judea where Zechariah lived, entered his house and greeted Elizabeth. When Elizabeth heard Mary's greeting, the baby in her womb moved excitedly. Elizabeth became filled with the Holy Spirit and spoke up in a loud voice,

" How blessed are you among women! And how blessed is the child in your womb! But who am I, that the mother of my Lord should come to me? For as soon as the sound of your greeting reached my ears, the baby in my womb leaped for joy! Yes! you are blessed, because you have trusted that the promise THE LORD that was made to you will be fulfilled."

Then Mary said,

"My soul glorifies the Lord and my spirit rejoices in God my Savior, for he has been mindful of the humble state of his servant. (1 Samuel 2:1) From now on all generations will call me blessed, for the Mighty One has done great things for me— his name is holy. His mercy extends to those who fear him, (Psalm 103:17) from generation to generation. He has performed mighty deeds with his arm; he has scattered those who are proud in their inmost thoughts. He has brought down rulers from their thrones but has lifted the humble. He has filled the hungry with good things but has sent the rich away empty. He has helped his servant Israel, remembering to be merciful to Abraham and his descendants forever, just as he promised our ancestors."

Mary stayed with Elizabeth for about three months and then returned home.

The time arrived for Elizabeth to have her baby, and she gave birth to a son. Her neighbors and relatives heard how good THE LORD had been to her, and they rejoiced with her.

On the eighth day,[3] they came to do the child's circumcision. They were about to name him Zechariah, after his father, when his mother spoke up and said, "No, he is to be called John." They said to her, "None of your relatives has that name," and they made signs to his father to find out what he wanted him called. He motioned for a writing tablet, and to everyone's surprise he wrote, "His name is John." At that moment, his ability to speak returned, and his first words were a blessing to God. All their neighbors were awestruck; and throughout the hill country of Judea, people talked all about these things. Everyone who heard of them said to himself, "What is this child going to be?" For clearly the hand of THE LORD was with him.

His father Zechariah became filled with the Holy Spirit and spoke this prophecy:[4]

"Praise be to the Lord, the God of Israel, because he has come to his people and redeemed them. He has raised up a horn of salvation for us in the house of his servant David (as he said he would through his prophets of long ago), to bring deliverance from our enemies and from the hand of all who hate us; to show mercy to our ancestors and also to remember his holy covenant which he swore to our father Abraham: in order to rescue us from the hand of our enemies, and to enable us to serve him without fear being holy in right standing before him all our days. And you, my child, will be called a prophet of the Most High; for you will go on before the Lord to prepare the way for him, (Malachi 3:1) to give his people the understanding of salvation through the forgiveness of their sins, because of the tender mercy of our God, by which the rising sun will come to us from heaven to shine on those living in darkness and in the shadow of death,(Isaiah 9:2) to guide our feet into the path of peace."

The child grew and became strong in spirit, and he lived in the wilderness until the time came for him to appear in public to Israel.

Notes

1. *Being engaged in this society was the same as legally married however the marriage had not been consummated yet.*

2. *Jesus' given name was the Hebrew name, Yeshua*

3. *The Jewish community were very familiar with the ordinances handed down by Moses from God. Males were to be circumcised when eight days old. It turns out that blood clotting first begins on this day. In addition, a covenant of protection was being made.*

4. *A prophecy is something that was spoken by God and heard by man.*

2

The birth and Childhood of Jesus

Around this time, the Roman Emperor Augustus issued an order for a census to be taken throughout the Empire. This was the first of its kind, took place when Quirinius was governor of Syria. Everyone went to be registered in his own town. Joseph, because he was a descendant of David, went up from the town of Nazareth in Galilee to the town of David, called Bethlehem, which was in Judea to be registered with Mary to whom he was engaged(legally married), and who was pregnant. While they were there, the time came and she gave birth to her first child, a son. She wrapped him in swaddling cloth and laid him down in a manger (feeding trough), because there was no space for them in the living-quarters.

Some shepherds were tending their sheep near Bethlehem one night when an angel of THE LORD appeared to them, and the Shekinah (Glory/presence) of THE LORD shone around them. They were terrified; but the angel said to them, "Don't be afraid, because I am here to tell you really Good News that will bring great joy to all the people. This very day, in the town of David, there was born for you a Deliverer who is the Messiah (Savior), the Lord. This is how you will know: you will find a baby wrapped in swaddling and lying in a feeding trough." Suddenly, along with the angel was a vast army from heaven praising God:

"In the highest heaven, glory to God! And on earth, peace among people of good will!"

As soon as the angels left them and had gone back into

heaven; the shepherds said to one another, "Let's go over to Bethlehem and see what has happened that THE LORD has told us about." Hurrying off, they came and found Mary and Joseph, and the baby lying in the feeding trough. Upon seeing this, they let them know what they had been told about this child; and all who heard them were amazed by what the shepherds said. Mary treasured all these things and kept mulling them over in her heart. Meanwhile, the shepherds returned to their flocks, glorifying and praising God for everything they had heard and seen; it had been just as they had been told.

When he was eight days old it was time for his circumcision, he was given the name Jesus, which is what the angel had called him before his was conceived.

The time came for their purification[1] according to the Scriptures of Moses and they took him up to Jerusalem to dedicate him to THE LORD (as it is written in the Scriptures of THE LORD, "Every firstborn male is to be consecrated to THE LORD" (Exodus 13:2) and also to offer a sacrifice of a pair of doves or two young pigeons (Leviticus 12:1-6-7) as required.

At that time there was a man in Jerusalem named Simeon. He was a righteous person, very devout and waited eagerly for God to deliver Israel. The Holy Spirit was with him and it had been revealed to him by the Holy Spirit that he would not die before he had seen the Messiah of THE LORD. Prompted by the Spirit, he went into the Temple courts; and when the parents brought in the child Jesus to do for him what the Scriptures required, Simeon took him in his arms and made a blessing to God, and said,

"Sovereign Lord, as you have promised, you may now dismiss your servant in peace. For my eyes have seen your salvation, which you have prepared in the sight of all nations: a light of revelation for the Gentiles, and the glory of your people Israel."

Joseph and Mary marveled at what was said about him. Then Simeon blessed them and said to Mary; "This child is destined to cause the falling and rising of many in Israel, and to be a sign that will be spoken against, so that the thoughts of many will be revealed. A sword will pierce your own soul too."

There was also a prophet named Hannah there, a daughter of Penuel, of the tribe of Asher. She was a very old woman who had lived with her husband for seven years of marriage and had remained a widow ever since; now she was eighty-four. She never left the Temple grounds but worshipped there night and day, fasting and praying. She came by at that moment and began thanking God and speaking about the child to everyone who was waiting for Jerusalem to be liberated.

When Joseph and Mary had finished doing everything required by the Scriptures of The LORD, they returned home to Nazareth in Galilee.

Jesus grew, became strong, filled with wisdom and God's favor was upon him.

Every year Jesus' parents went to Jerusalem for the festival of Passover. When he was twelve years old, they went up for the festival, as custom required. But after the festival was over and when his parents returned, Jesus remained in Jerusalem. They didn't realize this; thinking that he was somewhere else in the caravan. They traveled an entire day on the road before they began searching for him among their relatives and friends. Failing to find him, they returned to Jerusalem to look for him. On the third day they found him. He was sitting in the Temple court among the rabbis, not only listening to them but questioning what they said; and everyone who heard him was astonished at his insight/understanding and his answers. When his parents saw him, they were shocked; and his mother said to him, "Son! Why did you do this to us? Your father and I have been terribly worried looking for you!" He said to them, "Why did you have to look for me? Didn't you know that I had to be involving myself in my Father's affairs?" But they didn't understand what he meant.

So, he went with them to Nazareth and was obedient to them.

LUKE; What He Said...

His mother stored up all these things in her heart. And Jesus grew both in wisdom and in stature, gaining favor both with other people and with God.

12

Notes:

1.   *Ritual purification was required anytime blood was issued from the body.*

3

~18 years later…John the Baptizer and Lineage of Jesus

The following occurred during the time when the Roman Emperor Tiberius was in his 15th year of rule:[1] The governor of Judea was Pontius Pilot, Herod was the ruler of Galilee, Herod's brother Philip was the ruler of Iturea and Tracontis. Lysanias was ruler of Abilene. Anan and Caiaphas were the high priests.

The word of God came to john, son of Zechariah in the desert to begin his ministry. John then went throughout the region of Jordan proclaiming a baptism of turning to God from sin in order to be forgiven. This was just as had been written in the book of the prophet Isaiah,

"The voice of someone crying out in the desert

'Prepare the way for THE LORD!

Make straight paths for him!

Every valley must be filled in, every mountain and hill leveled;

the winding roads must be straightened

and the rough ways made smooth.

Then all humanity will see God's deliverance.'" (Isaiah 40:3-5)

John said to the crowds who came out to be baptized by him, "You snakes! Who warned you to escape the coming punishment? If you have really turned from your sins, do something that will prove it! And don't start saying to yourselves, 'Abraham is our father'! For I tell you that God can raise up for Abraham, sons from these stones! Already the axe is at the root of the trees, ready to strike; every tree that doesn't produce good fruit will be cut down and thrown into the fire!"

Some in the crowds asked John, "So then, what should we do?" He answered, "Whoever has two coats should share with somebody who has none, and whoever has food should do the same." Tax-collectors also came to be baptized; and they asked him, "Rabbi, what should we do?" "Collect no more than the government requires," he told them. Some soldiers asked him, "What about us? What should we do?" To them he said, "Don't intimidate anyone, don't accuse people falsely, and be satisfied with your pay."

The people were in a state of great expectancy, and everyone was wondering whether perhaps John himself might be the Messiah; so John addressed them, "I am baptizing you in water, but he who is coming is more powerful than I; I'm not even worthy to untie his sandals! He will baptize you in the Holy Spirit and in fire. He has with him his winnowing fork to clear out his threshing floor and gather his wheat into his barn, but he will burn up the straw with unquenchable fire!" With many other warnings besides these he proclaimed the Good News to the people.

John had denounced Herod who was the regional governor for taking as his own wife, Herodias, the wife of his brother, and for all the other wicked things Herod had done; at which point Herod added to his bad deeds by locking up John in prison.

While all the people were being baptized, Jesus too was baptized. As he was praying, heaven opened up and the Holy Spirit came down on him in physical form like a dove; and a voice from heaven was heard, "You are my Son, whom I love; I am very pleased with you."

Jesus was about thirty years old when he began his public ministry. The full lineage of Jesus is listed in the Gospel of Luke. It shows the Lineage from Adam to Jesus.[2]

Notes

1   *During this time in history the Romans ruled most of the Middle-East including the modern area of Israel which included Jerusalem.*

2   *The full lineage of Jesus is listed at the end of Chapter 3 in the Gospel of Luke. It shows his Lineage from Adam to Jesus. Jesus was about thirty years old when he began his public ministry.*

4

Jesus is tested, then begins his ministry of preaching and healing.

Then Jesus, filled with the Holy Spirit, returned from the Jordan river and was led by the Spirit in the wilderness for forty days of testing by the Adversary (Satan). During that time, he ate nothing, and afterwards he was hungry. The Adversary said to him, "If you are the Son of God, order this stone to become bread." Jesus replied, "The Scriptures says, 'Man does not live on bread alone.'" (Deuteronomy 8:3)

The Adversary took him up, showed him in an instant all the kingdoms of the world, and said to him, "I will give you authority and power over all of these. It has been handed over to me, and I can give it to whomever I want. Then if you will worship me, it will be all yours." Jesus answered him, "The Scriptures say, 'Worship THE LORD your God and serve him only.'" (Deuteronomy 6:14)

Then he took him to Jerusalem, set him on the highest point of the Temple and said to him, "If you are the Son of God, jump down from here! For the Scriptures say,

'He will order his angels to watch over you and to protect you. They will support you with their hands, they will support you with their hands, so that you will not hurt your feet on the stones.'" (Psalm 91:11,12)

Jesus said to him, "It also says, 'Do not put THE LORD your God to the test.'" (Deuteronomy 6:16)

When the Adversary had finished testing Jesus, he let him

alone until he had another opportunity.

Jesus returned to Galilee in the power of the Spirit, and reports about him spread throughout the countryside. He taught in their synagogues (Places of worship and learning), and everyone respected him.

He then went to Nazareth, where he had been brought up. On the Sabbath he went to the synagogue as usual. He stood up to read, and he was given the scroll of the prophet Isaiah. Unrolling the scroll, he found the place where it was written,

> *"The Spirit of THE LORD is upon me; because he has anointed me to announce Good News to the poor; he has sent me to proclaim freedom for the imprisoned and renew sight for the blind, to release those who have been crushed, to proclaim a year of the favor of THE LORD."* (Isaiah61:1,2 58:6)

 After closing the scroll and returning it to the attendant, he sat down; and the eyes of everyone in the synagogue were fixed on him. He began by saying to them; "Today, as you heard it read, this passage of the Scriptures was fulfilled!" Everyone was speaking well of him and marveling that such persuasive words were coming from his mouth. They were even asking, "How can this be Joseph's son?"

Jesus then said to them, "No doubt you will quote this proverb to me. '"Doctor, cure yourself!" The people said, 'We've heard about all the things that have been going on over in Capernaum; now do them here in your home town!' Yes!" He said, "I tell you that no prophet is accepted in his home town. It's true, I'm telling you that when Elijah was in Israel, and the sky was sealed off for three and a half years, so that there was a severe famine throughout the land, there were many widows; but Elijah was sent to none of them, only to a widow in Sarepta in the land of Sidon. Also, there were many people with leprosy in Israel during the time of the prophet Elisha; but not one of them was healed, only Naaman the Syrian."

On hearing this, everyone in the synagogue was filled with fury. They rose up, drove him out of town and dragged him to the edge of the cliff on which their town was built, intending to throw him off. But he walked right through the middle of the crowd and left there.

He went down to Capernaum, a town in the Galilee region and made a practice of teaching them on the Sabbath. They were amazed at the way he taught, because his words had authority.

In the synagogue there was a man who had a demonic spirit, who shouted in a loud voice, "What do you want with us, Jesus from Nazareth? Have you come to destroy us? I know who you are … the Holy One of God!" But Jesus rebuked it: "Be quiet and come out of him!" The demonic spirit threw the man down in the middle of the crowd and came out of him. They were all astounded and said to one another, "What kind of teaching is this? Why, he even gives orders with power and authority to the unclean spirits, and they come out!" Reports about him went out through the entire surrounding areas.

After leaving the synagogue, he went to Simon's house. Simon's mother-in-law was suffering from a high fever, and they asked him to do something for her. So, standing over her, he rebuked the fever; and it left her. She immediately got up and began helping them.

When evening had come, all those who had people that were sick with various diseases brought them to Jesus, and he put his hands on each one of them and healed them; also, demons came out of many, crying, "You are the Son of God!" But, rebuking them, he did not permit them to say that they knew he was the Messiah.

In the morning, he left and went away to a remote place. The people looked for and came to him and would have kept him from leaving. He said to them, "I must announce the Good News of the Kingdom of God to the other towns too. this is why I was sent." He also spent time preaching in the synagogues of Judea.

Notes

5

Jesus continues his ministry and gathers his close disciples.
Jesus starts using simple stories to instruct His followers.

One day, while Jesus was standing on the shore of Lake Gennesaret there was a huge crowd pushing in to what he was saying. He noticed two boats pulled up on the beach that were left there. He got into one of the boats which belonged to a fisherman named Simon and asked him to put out a little way from shore. Jesus sat down and taught the people from the boat.

When he had finished speaking, he said to Simon, "Go out further and see what you can catch." Simon said, "We've worked hard all night long, Rabbi (spiritual teacher), and haven't caught a thing! But if you say so, we will go further out and let down our nets." They did this and took in so many fish that their nets began to tear. They waved to their partners in the other boat to come and help them and they came and filled both boats to the point that they might sink. When he saw this, Simon prostrated himself in front of Jesus and said, "Get away from me, sir, because I'm a sinner!" because Simon and everyone near them were astonished by the catch of fish they had taken, including both James and John, Simon's partners. "Don't be frightened," Jesus said to Simon, "from now on you will be catching men!"[1] As soon as they had landed their boats, they left everything and followed him.

Once, when Jesus was in one of the towns, there came a man who was completely covered with leprosy.[2] On seeing Jesus, he fell on his face and begged him, "Sir, if you are willing, you can make me clean." Jesus reached out his hand and touched him, saying, "I am willing! Be healed!" Immediately the leprosy left him. Jesus warned him not to tell anyone. "Instead, as a testimony to the people, go straight to the priest and make an offering for your healing as Moses commanded." Despite the warning, the news about Jesus kept spreading all the more, so that huge crowds would gather to listen and be healed of their sicknesses. Jesus made a practice of withdrawing to remote places in order to pray.

One day when Jesus was teaching, there were Pharisees and Scripture-teachers present who had come from villages in Galilee and Judea, as well as from Jerusalem. The power of God the Father was with Jesus to heal the sick. One time, some men brought a paralyzed man lying on a bed. They wanted to bring him inside and lay him down in front of Jesus, but they couldn't find a way to get him in because of the crowd. So, they went up onto the roof and lowered him on his mattress after removing some roof tiles into the middle of the gathering, right in front of Jesus. When Jesus saw their trust(faith), he said, "Friend, your sins are forgiven." The Scripture-teachers and the Pharisees began thinking, "Who is this fellow that speaks such blasphemies? Who can forgive sin except God?" Jesus knew what they were thinking, said to them, "Why are you mulling such thoughts in your hearts? Is it easier to say 'your sins are forgiven' or 'Get up and walk'? Pay attention now, I'm going prove to you that the Son of Man[3] has authority on earth to forgive sins." He then said to the paralytic, "Get up, pick up your mattress and go home!" Immediately, in front of everyone, he stood up, picked up what he had been lying on, and went home praising God. Everyone was totally amazed, and they praised God; they were awestruck, saying, "We have seen extraordinary things today."[4]

Later on, Jesus saw a tax-collector named Levi sitting in his tax-collection[5] booth; and he said to him, "Follow me!" He got up, left everything and followed him.

Levi then gave a banquet at his house in Jesus' honor, and there was a lot of tax- collectors and others at the table with them. The

Pharisees and their Scripture-teachers complained about his disciples, saying, "Why do you eat and drink with tax-collectors and sinners?" It was Jesus who answered them: "The ones who need a doctor aren't the healthy but the sick. I have not come to call the 'righteous,' but rather to call sinners to turn to God from their sinful ways."

Next, they said to him, "John's disciples are always fasting and meditating on Scripture, and so are the disciples of the Pharisees; but your disciples go on eating and drinking." Jesus said to them, "Can you make wedding guests fast while the bridegroom is still with them? The time will come when the bridegroom will be taken away from them; and when that time comes, they will fast." Then he gave them an illustration: "No one tears a piece from a new coat and puts it on an old one; if he does, the new one will continue to rip, but the piece from the new one will not match the old. Also, no one puts new wine into old wineskins; if he does, the new wine ferment and will burst the skins and be spilled, and those skins will also be ruined. On the contrary, new wine must be put into fresh new wineskins. Besides that, after drinking old wine, people don't want the new; because they say, 'The old is good enough.'"

Notes

1. *Jesus was telling Simon that instead of catching fish, he could be drawing people to God.*

2. *Leprosy is a severe form of psoriasis that was highly contagious. Severe to the point of losing appendages because of this. There was no cure at this time in history.*

3. *"Son of Man" was the title Jesus used when referring to himself.*

4. *Jesus always equated physical healing with salvation, repentance and the forgiveness of sins.*

5. *Tax collectors were despised by the common people because they were acting as agents for the Roman Empire. They were often corrupt and protected by the Roman Rulers.*

6

Jesus begins issuing dire warnings to the religious establishment using parables.

On one Sabbath,[1] while Jesus was passing through some wheat fields, his disciples began plucking the heads of grain, rubbing them between their hands and eating the seeds. Some of the Pharisees said, "Why are you violating the Sabbath?" Jesus said, "Haven't you ever read what David did when he and his companions were hungry? He entered the House of God(temple) and took and ate the Bread of the Presence" which no one is permitted to eat but the priest. "The Son of Man," he concluded, "is Lord of the Sabbath."

On another Sabbath, when Jesus had gone into the synagogue and was teaching, a man with a shriveled hand was there. The Scripture-teachers and Pharisees watched Jesus carefully to see if he would heal on the Sabbath so that they could accuse him of something. But he knew what they were thinking and said to the man, "Come up and stand where we can see you!" He got up and stood there. Then Jesus said to them, "I ask you: what is permitted on the Sabbath? Doing good or doing evil? Saving life or destroying it?" Then after looking around at all of them, he said to the man, "Hold out your hand." Then as he held it out, his hand was restored to normal. The others became angry and began discussing with each other what they could do to Jesus.

It was around that time that Jesus went out to the hill country to pray, and all night he prayed continuously. When day came, he called his disciples and twelve were chosen to be known as emissaries (apostles/sent ones):

Simon, whom he named Peter; Andrew, his brother; Jacob; John; Philip; Bartholomew; Matthew; Thomas; James son of Alphaeus; Simon, the one called the Zealot; Judas brother of James; and Judas from Iscariot, who turned traitor.

Then he came down with them and stood on a flat area. A large crowd of his disciples was there with great numbers of people from all over Judea, Jerusalem and the coast around Tyre and Sidon. They had come to hear him and be healed of their diseases. Those who were troubled with unclean spirits were being healed; and the whole crowd was trying to touch him, because power kept going out from him, healing everyone. He looked at his disciples and said:

"Blessed are you who are poor (in spirit), for yours is the kingdom of God. Blessed are you who hunger(spiritually) now, for you will be satisfied. "How blessed are you who are crying now! for you will laugh. "How blessed you are whenever people hate you and ostracize you and insult you and denounce you as a criminal on my account. Be glad when that happens; yes, dance for joy! because in heaven your reward is great. For that is just how their fathers treated3 the prophets.

"What sorrow awaits you who are rich, for you have already received your comfort. What sorrow awaits you who are well fed now, for you will go hungry. What sorrow awaits you who laugh now, for you will mourn and weep. What sorrow awaits you when everyone speaks well of you, for that is how their ancestors treated the false prophets.[3] What sorrow awaits you when people speak well of you, for that is just how their fathers treated the false prophets!"

"But to you who are listening I say: Love your enemies, do good to those who hate you, bless those who curse you, pray for those who mistreat you. If someone hits you on one cheek, offer the other too; If someone takes your coat, give him your shirt as well.

If someone asks you for something, give it to him, if someone takes what belongs to you, don't demand it back. "Treat other people as you would like them to treat you. What credit is it to you if you love only those who love you? Even sinners love those who love them. What credit is it to you if you do good only to those who do good to you? Even sinners do that. What credit is it to you if you lend only to those who you expect will pay you back? Even sinners lend to each other, expecting to be repaid in full. Love your enemies, do good, and lend expecting nothing back! Your reward will be great, and you will be children of The Most High; for he is kind to the ungrateful and the wicked. Show compassion, just as your Father shows compassion. "Don't judge, and you won't be judged. Don't condemn, and you won't be condemned. Forgive, and you will be forgiven. Give and you will receive gifts; the full measure, compacted, shaken together and overflowing, will be given to you. For the measure with which you give out will be used to measure back to you!" He also told them a parable: "Can one blind man lead another blind man? Won't they both fall into a pit? A disciple is not above his rabbi(teacher); but each one, when he is fully trained, will be like his rabbi. So why do you see the splinter in your brother's eye, but not notice the log in your own eye? How can you say to your brother, 'Brother, let me help you get that splinter out of your eye,' when you yourself don't see the log in your own eye? You hypocrite! First take the log out of your own eye; then you will see clearly, so that you can remove the splinter from your brother's eye!

"No good tree produces bad fruit, nor does a bad tree produce good fruit. Each tree is recognized by its own fruit; figs aren't picked from thorn bushes or grapes from a briar patch. A good person produces good things from the goodness in his heart, while an evil person produces evil things from what is stored in his heart. A person speaks what overflows from his heart.

"Why do you call me, 'Lord! Lord!' but don't do what I say? Everyone who comes to me, hears my words and acts on them, I will show you what he is like: he is like someone building a house who dug deep and laid the foundation on bedrock. When a flood came, the torrent beat against the house but couldn't move it because it was constructed on a solid foundation. And whoever hears my words but doesn't act on them is like someone who built his house on the ground without any foundation. As soon as the waters struck it, it collapsed and that house it collapsed!"

Notes

1. *The sabbath was the one day set aside by God for resting and not working. It was a time for family and honoring God. Of course, when humans get involved, they usually take things to the extreme. Well-meaning leaders came up with many different rules so people would not violate the Sabbath. These rules became more important than the actual Sabbath.*

2. *The leaders were angry because Jesus was showing them up, showing how they were more concerned with legalism than compassion and mercy.*

3. *Repeatedly through the ages, God would send Prophets to warn the people that they needed to change their ways or suffer disaster. Most times the people would not listen and sometimes murdered the Prophets of God.*

7

A Roman soldier knows Jesus has authority. Jesus raises a man from the dead, then dines with a Pharisee

When Jesus had finished speaking to the people, he went back to Capernaum. A Roman army officer there had a servant that he regarded highly and who was sick and near death. Hearing about Jesus, the officer had some Jewish elders go to him with the request that he come and heal his servant. They came to Jesus and pleaded earnestly with him, "He really deserves to have you do this because he loves our people, in fact, he is the one that built the synagogue for us!" Jesus then proceeded to go with them. He had not gone far from the house, when the officer sent friends who said to him, "Sir, don't trouble yourself. I'm not worthy to have you come into my home which is why I didn't presume to approach you myself. Instead, just give a command and have my servant recover. I too am a man set under authority. I have soldiers under me; and I say to this one, 'Go!' and he goes; and to another, 'Come!' and he comes; and to my servant, 'Do this!' and he does it." Jesus was astonished when he heard this and he turned and said to the crowd following him, "not even in Israel have I found such trust!" When the messengers got back to the officer's house, they found the servant in good health.

The next day Jesus along with his disciples and a large crowd went to a town called Nain. As he approached the town gate, a dead man was being carried out for burial. His mother was a widow and was her only son[1]. A large crowd from the town was with her. When the Lord saw her, he felt compassion for her and said to her, "Don't cry." Then he came close and touched the coffin, and the pallbearers halted. He said, "Young man, get up!" The dead man sat up and began to speak, and Jesus presented him to his mother. (1Kings 17:23) Everyone was filled with awe and gave glory to God, saying, "A great prophet has appeared among us," and, "God has come to help his people." This story about him spread throughout all Judea and the surrounding countryside.

John's disciples informed him of all these things. Then John spoke to two of his disciples and sent them to the Lord to ask, "Are you the one who is to come, or should we look for someone else?" When the men came to Jesus, they said, "John the Baptizer has sent us to you to ask, 'Are you the one who is to come? Or should we keep looking for someone else?'[2] "At that moment he was healing many people of diseases, pains, evil spirits, and giving sight to many who were blind. So he answered them by saying, "Go tell John what you have been seeing and hearing: the blind are seeing again, the lame are walking, (Isaiah 35:5,6) people with leprosy are being healed, the deaf are hearing, (Isaiah 35:6) the dead are being raised (back to life), the Good News is being told to the poor (Isaiah 61:1) and how blessed is anyone who is not offended by me!"

When the messengers from John had gone, Jesus spoke to the crowds about John: "What did you go out into the desert to see? Reeds swaying in the breeze? No? Then what did you go out to see? Someone who was well dressed? No people who dress beautifully and live in luxury are found in kings' palaces. Well then, what did you go out to see? A prophet! Yes, and I tell you he is much more than a prophet. This is the one about whom the Scriptures say,

> *'See, I am sending out my messenger before you; he will prepare your way before you.'* (Malachi 3:1)

I'm telling you that of those born of women, there has not risen anyone greater than John the Baptizer! Yet the one who is least in the Kingdom of Heaven is greater than he!"

All the people who heard him, even the tax-collectors, being baptized by John, acknowledged that God's way was right; but the Pharisees and the Scripture-teachers, by not letting themselves be baptized by him, nullified for themselves God's plan.

"Therefore," said the Lord, "how can I describe the people of this generation? What are they like? They are like children sitting in the marketplaces, calling to one another,

'We made happy music, but you wouldn't dance! We made sad music, but you wouldn't cry!'

John came and he does not eat bread or drink wine; and you say, 'He has a demon!' The Son of Man has come eating and drinking; and you say, 'Aha! A glutton and a drunk! A friend of tax-collectors and sinners!' Well, the proof of wisdom is in all the people it produces."

One of the Pharisees invited Jesus to eat with him, and he went into the home of the Pharisee and took his place at the table. A woman who lived in that town and was living a sinful life, was aware that he was eating in the home of the Pharisee, brought an alabaster box of very expensive perfume, stood behind Jesus at his feet and wept until her tears began to wash his feet. Then she wiped his feet with her own hair, kissed his feet and poured the perfume on them.

When the Pharisee who had invited him, saw what was going on, he said to himself, "If this man were really a prophet, he would have known who is touching him and what sort of woman she is, a sinner." Jesus answered his thought, "Simon, I have something to say to you." "Say it, Rabbi," he replied. "A certain creditor had two debtors and one owed ten times as much as the other. When they were unable to pay him back, he canceled both their debts. Now which of them will love him more?" Simon answered, "I suppose the one for whom he forgave the larger debt." "You have judged correctly," Jesus said to him.

Then, turning to the woman, he said to Simon, "Do you see this woman? I came into your house and you didn't give me water for my feet, but this woman has washed my feet with her tears and dried them with her hair! You didn't give me a kiss; but from the time I came in, this woman has not stopped kissing my feet! You didn't put oil on my head, but this woman poured perfume on my feet! Because of this, I say of her sins; which are many! they have been forgiven because she loved much. But someone who has been forgiven only a little, loves only a little." Then he said to her, "Your sins have been forgiven." At this, those eating with him began saying among themselves, "Who is this person that presumes to forgive sins?" Then he said to the woman, "Your trust has saved you; go in peace."

NOTES

1. *This only son was here only provider as her husband had died. He would take care of her through her old age.*

2. *The Jews were waiting expectantly for the Messiah to come and deliver them from Roman rule.*

8

Jesus travels from town to town Rebukes a Storm. Heals a demoniac and a woman. Raises a girl.

Jesus then traveled about from town to town and village to village, publicly announcing the Good News of the Kingdom of God. With him were the Twelve, and several women who had been healed from evil spirits and illnesses. Mary (called Magdalene), from whom seven demons had come out; Joanna the wife of Herod's finance minister, Chuza; Susanna; and many other women who drew on their own wealth to help him.

After a large crowd had gathered who had come to him to him from each town, Jesus told this parable: "A farmer went out to plant his seed. As he sowed it, some fell along the footpath and was stepped on, and the birds flying around ate it up. Some fell on rock; and after it sprouted, it dried up from lack of moisture. Some fell among thorns, and the thorns grew up with it and choked it out. But some fell into rich soil, and grew, and produced a hundred times as much as had been sown." After saying this, he shouted out, "Whoever has ears to hear with, let him hear!"

His disciples asked him what this parable might mean, and he said, "To you it has been given to know the secrets of the Kingdom of God; but the rest are taught in parables, so that they may look but do not see, and listen but not understand. (Isaiah 6:9)

"The parable meaning is this: the seed is God's message. The ones along the path are those who hear, but then the Adversary comes and takes the message out of their hearts, in order to keep them from being saved by trusting it. The ones on rock are those who, when they hear the word, accept it with joy; but these have no root in themselves, they go on trusting for a while; but when a time of testing comes, they turn away. As for what fell among the thorns are the ones who hear; but as they go along, worries and wealth and life's pleasures crowd in and choke them, so that their fruit never matures. But what fell in rich soil, these are the ones who, when they hear the message, hold onto it with a good, receptive heart; treasure it and bring forth a harvest.

"No one who has lit a lamp would cover it with a bowl or put it under a bed; no, he puts it on a table or stand; so that those coming in may see the light. For everything that is hidden will be known, anything that is covered up will be known and made public. Pay attention to how you hear! For anyone who has something will be given more; but from anyone who has nothing, even what he seems to have will be taken away."

Then Jesus' mother and brothers came to see him, but they couldn't get near him because of the crowd. It was reported to him, "Your mother and your brothers are standing outside and want to see you." But he gave them this answer: "My mother and brothers are those who hear God's message and act on it!"

One day Jesus got into a boat with his disciples and said to them, "Let's cross to the other side of the lake." So, they set out; and as they were sailing, he fell asleep. A windstorm came down on the lake, so that the boat began to fill up with water and putting them in great danger. They went and woke him up, saying, "Rabbi! Rabbi! We're about to die!" He woke up, rebuked the wind and the rough water; and they calmed down and became still. Then he said to the disciples, "Where is your trust?" In awe, they marveled, asking one another, "Who can this be, that he commands the wind and the water, and even they obey him?"

They kept on sailing and landed in the region of the Gadarenes, which is opposite the region of Galilee. As Jesus stepped ashore, a man from the town who had demons came to meet him. He had not worn clothes for a very long time; he did not live in a house, but in the burial caves. Catching sight of Jesus, he screamed, fell down in front of him and yelled, "Jesus! Son of God The Most High! What do you want with me? I beg you, don't torture me!" because Jesus had ordered the unclean spirit to come out of the man. It had often taken hold of him and he had been watched over and guarded, chained hand and foot, but had broken the chains and been driven by the demon into the desert. Jesus asked him, "What is your name?" speaking to the man, not the demons "Legion," he said, because many demons had entered him. They begged Jesus not to order them to go off into the Bottomless Pit. The place of final punishment.

Now there was a herd of many pigs, feeding on the hill; and the demons begged him to let them go into these. He then gave them permission. The demons came out of the man and entered the pigs, whereupon the herd rushed down the hillside into the lake and drowned.

When the pig farmers saw what had happened, they fled and told it in the town and in the country; and the people came out to see for themselves. They came to Jesus and found the man that the demons had left, sitting dressed and in his right mind at the feet of Jesus; and they were frightened. Those who had seen it told how the formerly demonized man had been set free.

Then all the people of the Gerasene district asked him to leave them, for they had been seized with great fear. He then boarded the boat and returned. The man from whom the demons had gone out of begged that he might go with him; but Jesus sent him away, saying, "Go back to your home and tell how much God has done for you." He went away proclaiming throughout the whole town how much Jesus had done for him.

When Jesus got back, the crowd welcomed him; because they were all expecting him. There came a man named Jairus who was head of the synagogue. Falling at Jesus' feet, he pleaded with him to come to his house; because he only had one daughter, about twelve years old; who she was dying.

As he went, the crowds on every side were virtually crushing him, a woman who had a hemorrhage (bleeding ulcer) for twelve years, and could not be healed by anyone, came up behind him and touched the tassel(wing) on his robe; instantly her hemorrhaging stopped. Jesus asked, "Who touched me?" When they all denied doing it, Peter said, "Rabbi! The crowds are hemming you in and jostling you!" But Jesus said, "Someone did touch me, because I felt power go out of me." Seeing she could not leave un-noticed, the woman, trembling with fear, threw herself down before him and confessed in front of everyone why she had touched him and how she had been instantly healed. He said to her, "My daughter, your trust has saved you; go in peace."

While Jesus was still speaking, a man came from the synagogue president's house. "Your daughter has died," he said. "Don't bother the rabbi anymore." But on hearing this, Jesus said to him, "Don't be afraid! Just go on trusting, and she will be made well." When he arrived at the house, he didn't allow anyone to go in with him except Peter, John, James and the child's father and mother All the people were wailing and mourning for her; Jesus said, "Don't weep; she hasn't died, she just sleeping." They jeered at him, since they knew she had died. But he took her by the hand, called out, "Little girl, get up!" and her spirit returned. She stood up at once, and he instructed that something she be given something to eat. Her parents were astounded, he told them to tell no one what had happened.

9

Calling the Twelve disciples together, Jesus gave them power and authority to expel all demons and to cure diseases; then he sent them out to announce the Kingdom of God and to heal the sick. He then said to them, "Don't bring anything with you for your trip, not even a walking stick or a pack, neither food nor money; and don't bring two shirts. Whatever house you enter, stay there while you go in and out from there. Wherever they don't welcome you, shake the dust from your feet when you leave that town as a warning to them." They set out and went through village after village, healing and announcing the Good News everywhere.

Herod the governor had heard about all that was going on and was perplexed, because it was said by some that John(the Baptizer) had been raised from the dead,   others said that (the prophet)Elijah had appeared, and by others that one of the prophets of long ago had come back to life. Herod said, "I had John beheaded, so who is this I keep hearing about?" And he began trying to meet him.

On their return, the twelve disciples told Jesus what they had done. Then taking them with him, he withdrew to a town called Bethsaida.   When the crowds found out, they followed him. Welcoming them, he spoke to them about the Kingdom of God and to heal those who needed to be healed.

As the day came to an end, the twelve disciples came to him and said, "Send the crowd away, so that they can go and get lodging and food in the towns and farms around here, because we are is a remote place." He said to them, "You give them something to eat!" They replied, "We only have five loaves of bread and two fish, unless we are supposed to go and buy food for all these people!" (there were about five thousand men.) He said to his disciples, "Make them sit down in groups of around fifty." They did what he told them and had them all sit down. Then he took the five loaves and the two fish and looking up to heaven, He made a blessing, then broke the loaves and began giving them to the disciples to distribute to the crowd. Everyone ate as much as he wanted; and they took up what was left over which was twelve baskets full of pieces.

Once when Jesus was praying quietly and his disciples were with him; he asked them, "Who do the people say I am?" They replied, "John the Baptizer; but others say Elijah, and others that some prophet of long ago has risen." "But you," he said to them, "who do you say I am?" Peter replied, "The Messiah of God!" However, Jesus, warned and ordered them not to tell anyone, then added, "The Son of Man has to go through terrible suffering and be rejected by the elders, the head priest and Scripture-teachers; and he has to be put to death; but on the third day, he has to be raised back to life."

Then to everyone else he said, "If anyone wants to follow me, let him deny himself, take up his own cross each day and continue following me. For whoever tries to save his own life will destroy it, but whoever loses his life on my account will save it.[1] What will it benefit a person if he gains the whole world but destroys or forfeits his own life? If someone is ashamed of me and of what I say, the Son of Man will be ashamed of him (deny him) when he comes in his glory and that of the Father and of the holy angels. I 'm telling you a truth, there are some people standing here who will not die until they see the Kingdom of God."

About a week after Jesus said these things, he took Peter, John and James with him and went up to the hill country to pray. As he was praying, the appearance of his face changed; and his clothing became a dazzling white. Suddenly there were two men talking with him; Moses and Elijah. They appeared in glorious splendor and spoke of his exodus,[2] which he was soon to accomplish in Jerusalem. Peter and those with him had been sound asleep; but when they woke up, they saw his glory and the two men standing with him. As the men were leaving Jesus, Peter said to him, not knowing what he was saying, "It's good that we're here, Rabbi! Let us build three shelters as memorials; one for you, one for Moses and one for Elijah." As Peter spoke, a cloud came and enveloped them. They were frightened as the cloud covered them; and a voice came out of the cloud, saying, "This is my Son, whom I have chosen. Listen to him!" When the voice stopped, Jesus was alone again. They kept it secret and told no one at that time of anything they had seen.

The next day, as they were coming down out of the hill country, a large crowd met him. Suddenly a man in the crowd shouted, "Rabbi! Look at my son, I beg you, because he's my only child! Here is what happens to him: a spirit seizes him, makes him shriek and throws him into convulsions with foaming at the mouth… only rarely will it leave him. It's destroying him! I asked your disciples to drive the spirit out, but they couldn't." "Perverted people, without any trust!" Jesus answered, "How long do I have to be with you and put up with you? Bring your son here." Even as the boy was coming, the demon threw him to the ground and caused him to convulse. But Jesus rebuked the unclean spirit, healed the boy and gave him back to his father. Everyone was amazement at the greatness of God. While all of them were still marveling at everything Jesus was doing, he said to his disciples, "Listen very carefully to what I'm going to say. The Son of Man is about to be betrayed into the hands of men." But they didn't understand what he meant by this. It had been hidden from them so that they would not grasp its meaning, and they were afraid to ask him about it.

An argument arose among the disciples as to which of them might be the greatest. Jesus, knowing the thoughts of their hearts, took a child and stood him beside him, said to them, "Whoever welcomes this child in my name welcomes me, and whoever welcomes me welcomes the One who sent me. In other words, the one who is least among you, is the one who is greatest." John responded, "Rabbi, we saw someone expelling demons in your name; so, we stopped him because he is not part of our group. Jesus said to him, "Don't stop such people, because whoever isn't against you is for you."

As the time approached for him to be taken up into heaven, he made his decision to head out to Jerusalem. He sent messengers ahead of him, that went and entered a village in Samaria to prepare for him. But the people of that village would not let him stay there, because his destination was Jerusalem. When the disciples James and John saw this, they said, "Sir, do you want us to call down fire from heaven to destroy them?" (2Kings 1:10) however Jesus turned and rebuked them. Then they went on to another village.

As they were traveling on the road, a man said to him, "I will follow you wherever you go." Jesus replied to him, "The foxes have holes, and the birds have nests, but the Son of Man has no (earthly) home of his own." To another he said, "Follow me!" but the man replied, "Sir, first let me go and bury my father." Jesus said, "Let the dead bury their own dead;[3] you, go and proclaim the Kingdom of God!" Yet another said, "I will follow you sir, but first let me say good-by to the people at home." To him Jesus said, "No one who puts his hand to the plow and keeps looking back is fit to serve in the Kingdom of God."

Notes

1. *Jesus is referring to everlasting life of the human spirit, who a person is that lives forever. The question is where will you spend eternity.*

2. *Jesus was discussing his death and following resurrection.*

3. *There was a custom that approximately a year after burial, when the flesh was gone, the bones would be moved to a permanent location. This second burial was a common custom.*

LUKE; What He Said...

10

After this, the Lord appointed seventy other disciples and sent them on ahead in pairs to every town and place where he was about to go. He said to them, "To be sure, there is a large harvest. But there are so few workers. Therefore, plead with the Lord of the Harvest that he quickly send workers out to gather in his harvest. Get going now but pay attention! I am sending you out like lambs among wolves. Don't carry a money-belt or a pack, and don't stop to idly chat with people on the road.

"Whenever you enter a house, first say, 'peace!' to the household. If a lover of peace is there, your 'Peace!' will find its rest with him; and if not, it will return to you. Stay in that same house, eating and drinking what they offer because a worker deserves his wages. Don't move about from house to house.

"Whenever you come into a town where they make you welcome, eat whatever they prepare for you. Heal the sick there, and tell them, 'The Kingdom of God is near you.' But whenever you enter a town and they don't make you welcome, go out into its streets and say, 'Even the dust of your town that sticks to our feet; we shake off as a sign against you! But understand this: The Kingdom of God is near!' I tell you; it will be more tolerable on the Day of Judgment for Sodom than for that town.

"Woe to you, Chorazin! Woe to you, Bethsaida! For if the miracles done in you had been done in Tyre and Sidon, they would long ago have put on sackcloth and ashes as evidence that they had repented and changed their ways. But at the Judgment it will be more bearable for Tyre and Sidon than for you!

"And you, Capernaum, will you be exalted to heaven? No, you will be brought down to the place of the dead! (Isaiah 14:14,15)

"Whoever listens to you, listens to me. Also, whoever rejects you, rejects me; whoever rejects me rejects the One who sent me."

The seventy came back thrilled and delighted. "Lord," they said, "with your power, even the demons submit to us!" Jesus said to them, "I saw Satan fall like lightning from heaven. Remember, I have given you authority so that you can trample snakes and scorpions, in fact, all the Enemy; and you will remain completely unharmed. Don't be glad that the spirits submit to you; be glad that your names have been recorded in heaven."

At that moment he was filled with joy by the Holy Spirit and said, "Father, Lord of heaven and earth, I thank you because you concealed these things from the intellectuals and the educated, but You revealed them to ordinary people. Yes, Father, I thank you that it pleased you to do this.

"My Father has handed over everything to me. Indeed, no one fully knows who the Son is except the Father, and who the Father is except the Son and those to whom the Son wishes to reveal Him." Then, turning to the disciples, he said privately, "How blessed are the eyes that see what you are seeing! Without doubt, many prophets and kings wanted to see the things you are seeing but did not get to see them, and to hear the things you are hearing, but did not hear them."

An expert in Scripture stood up to try and trap him by asking, "Rabbi, what should I do to obtain eternal life?" Jesus said to him, "What is written in the Scriptures? How do you read it?" He answered, "You are to love THE LORD your God with all your heart, with all your soul, with all your strength and with all your understanding; and love your neighbor as yourself." (Deuteronomy 6:5) "That's the right answer," Jesus said. "Do this, and you will have eternal life."

But he, trying to justify himself, said to Jesus, "So who is my 'neighbor'?" Addressing the question, Jesus said: "A man was traveling from Jerusalem to Jericho when he was attacked by robbers. They stripped him naked and beat him up, then left, leaving him half dead. By chance, a priest was going down on that road; but when he saw him, he passed by on the other side. Likewise, a Levi who reached the same place and saw him also passed by on the other side.

"Then a man from Samaria[1] who was traveling came upon him; and when he saw him, he was moved with compassion. So, he went to him, put oil and wine on his wounds and bandaged them. Then he set him on his own donkey, brought him to an inn and took care of him. The next day, he took out two days' wages, gave them to the innkeeper and said, 'Look after him; and if you spend more than this, I'll pay you back when I return.' Of these three, which one seems to you to have become the 'neighbor' of the man who fell among robbers?" He answered, "The one who showed mercy toward him." Jesus said to him, "You go and do the same."

On their way Jesus and his disciples came to a village where a woman named Martha who welcomed him into her home. She had a sister called Mary who also sat at the Lord's feet and heard what he had to say. But Martha was busy with all the work to be done; so, going up to him, she said, "Sir, don't you care that my sister has been leaving me to do everything by myself?" However, the Lord answered her, "Martha, Martha, you are fretting and worrying about so many things! But there is only one thing that is essential. Mary has chosen to do the right thing, and it will not be taken away from her."

Notes

1. *Samaritans were considered half-breeds by the Jews as they Jews that had intermarried with non-Jews. They were not allowed to associate with them.*

11

Jesus teaches his disciples how to pray. Jesus has more dire warnings for the religious leadership.

One time when Jesus was in a private place praying. As he finished, one of the disciples said to him, "Sir, teach us to pray, just as John taught his disciples." He said to them, "When you pray, say: 'Father, may your name be kept holy. May your kingdom come. Give us each day the food we need. Forgive us our sins, for we too forgive everyone who has wronged us. And do not lead us into hard testing.'

He also said to them, "Suppose one of you has a friend; and you go to him in the middle of the night and say to him, 'Friend, lend me three loaves of bread, because a friend of mine who is travelling has just arrived at my house, and I don't have anything for him to eat.' Now the man inside may answer, 'Don't bother me! The door is already shut, my children are with me in bed; I can't get up to give you anything!' But I tell you, even if he won't get up because the man is his friend, but because of the man's nerve/persistence he will get up and give him as much as he needs.

"In addition, I tell you: keep asking, and it will be given to you; keep seeking, and you will find; keep knocking, and the door will be opened to you. For everyone who goes on asking receives; and he who keeps on seeking finds; and to him who continues to knock, the door will be opened to him.

"Is there any father here who, if his son asked him for a fish, would instead of a fish give him a snake? or if he asked for an egg would give him a scorpion? Therefore, if you, even though you are bad, know how to give your children good gifts, how much more will the Father keep giving the Holy Spirit from heaven to those who keep asking him!"

When He had expelled a demon that was mute, and the demon had gone out of him, the mute man spoke; and the people were astounded. But some of them said, "It is by Beelzebub" the ruler of the demons "that he expels the demons." And others, trying to trap him, demanded from him a sign from Heaven. But he, knowing what they were thinking, said to them, "Every kingdom divided against itself will collapse, with one house falling on another. So, if the Adversary is also divided against himself, how can his kingdom survive? I'm asking because you claim it is by Beelzebub that I drive out the demons. If I drive out demons by Beelzebub, then by whom do your people drive them out? So, they will be your judges! But if I drive out demons by the finger of God, (Exodus 8:19) then the Kingdom of God has come upon you!

"When a strong man who is ready for battle guards his own house, his possessions are secure. But when someone stronger attacks and defeats him, carries off all the armor and weaponry on which the man was depending on and divides up the spoils. Those who are not with me are against me, and those who do not gather with me are working against me.

"When a demonic spirit comes out of a person, it travels through dry country looking for something to inhabit. When it does not find anything, it will say to itself, 'I'm going to return to the house I left.' When it arrives, if it finds the house swept clean and put in order. Then it will bring seven other spirits even more evil than itself and live there; so that in the end the person is much worse off than he was before."

As Jesus was saying these things, a woman in the crowd raised her voice an called out, "How blessed is the mother that gave birth to you and nursed you from her breast!" He responded, "So much more blessed are those who hear the word of God and obey it!"

As the people crowded around him, Jesus went on to say, "This generation is a wicked generation! It demands signs, but no sign will be given but the sign of Jonah.[1] For just as Jonah became a sign to the people of Nineveh, so will the Son of Man be for this generation. The Queen of the South (Sheba) will appear at the Judgment with the people of this generation and condemn them; for she came from far away to hear the wisdom of Solomon, and what is here now is greater than Solomon. The people of Nineveh will stand up at the Judgment with this generation and condemn it, for they turned to God from their sins when Jonah1 preached, and what is here now is greater than Jonah.

"No one who has lit a lamp hides it or places it under a bowl; rather, he puts it on a stand, so that those coming in may see its light. The lamp of your body is the eye. When you have a 'good eye,' (when you are generous,) your whole body is full of light; but when you have an 'evil eye,' (when you are stingy,) your body is full of darkness. So, take care that the light in you is not darkness! If, then, your whole body is filled with light, with no part dark, it will be fully lit, as when a bright lamp is shining on you."

As Jesus spoke, a Pharisee asked him to eat dinner with him; so, he went in and took his place at the table. The Pharisee was surprised that he didn't begin by doing ceremonial washing of his hands before the meal. However, the Lord said to him, "Now then, you Pharisees, you clean the outside of the cup and plate; but inside, you are full of robbery and wickedness. Fools! Didn't the One who made the outside make the inside too? Rather, give as alms what is inside, and then everything will be clean for you!

"But woe to you Pharisees! You pay your tithes[2] of every garden herb, but you ignore justice and the love of God. You have an obligation to do these things but without disregarding the others!

"Woe to you Pharisees, because you love the best seat in the synagogues and being greeted deferentially in the marketplaces!

"Woe to you, because you are like unmarked graves, which people walk over without knowing it."

One of the experts in Scriptures answered him, "Rabbi, by saying these things you are insulting us too." Jesus said, "How terrible it will be for you Scriptures experts too! You load people down with burdens they can hardly bear, and then you won't lift a finger to help them!

"Woe to you! You build tombs in memory of the prophets, but your fathers murdered them! Thus, you testify that you completely approve of what your fathers did; they did the killing and you build monuments to them! Therefore the Wisdom of God said, 'I will send them prophets and emissaries; they will kill some and persecute others'; so that on this generation will fall the responsibility for all the prophets' blood that has been spilled since the world was established, from the blood of Able to the blood of Zechariah, who was killed between the altar and the Holy Place. Yes, I tell you, the responsibility for it will fall on this generation!

"Great suffering awaits you Scriptures experts! For you have taken away the key of knowledge! Not only did you yourselves not go in, you also have stopped those who were trying to enter!"

As Jesus left that place, the Scripture-teachers and the Pharisees began to confront him and get him to express his views on all sorts of subjects, laying traps to catch him in something he might say.

Notes

1. *Jonah was a prophet sent to warn the city of Nineveh to change their ways or suffer disaster. They repented and were spared.*

2. *A tithe was the equivalent of 1/10. They were required to bring a 1/10 of their income in whatever form they had to the temple as a thanks or acknowledgement that God was responsible for blessing the work of their hands.*

12

Jesus tells his followers not to be afraid of men, because his Father in heaven cares for them. He then instructs them to be prepared.

Meanwhile, as a crowd numbering in the tens of thousands gathered so closely as to trample each other down, Jesus said to his disciples first, "Guard yourselves from the leavened bread of the Pharisees, by which I mean their hypocrisy (They themselves don't do what they teach). There is nothing covered up that will not be uncovered or hidden that will not become known. What you have spoken in the dark will be heard in the light, and what you have whispered behind closed doors will be proclaimed on the housetops.

My friends, I tell you: don't fear those who can kill the body and then nothing more. I will show you whom to fear: Fear him who after killing you has authority to throw you into Hell! Yes, I tell you, this is the one to fear! Aren't sparrows sold for next to nothing, five for two pennies? Yet not one of them is forgotten by God. Why, even every hair on your head has been counted! Don't be afraid, you are more valuable than many sparrows.

Also, I'm telling you, whoever acknowledges me in the presence of others, the Son of Man will also acknowledge in the presence of God's angels. But whoever disowns me before others will be disowned before the angels of God. Also, everyone who says something against the Son of Man will be forgiven; but whoever speaks evil of the Holy Spirit will not be forgiven.

When they bring you before the synagogues and those with

power and the authorities, don't worry about how you will defend yourself or what you will say; because when the time comes, the Holy Spirit will teach you what you should say."

Someone in the crowd said to him, "Rabbi, tell my brother to share our family inheritance with me." But Jesus replied him, "My friend, who appointed me judge or arbitrator over you?" He then turned to the people and said, "Take care to guard against all forms of greed, because even if someone is rich, his life does not consist in what he owns." And he told them this parable(illustration): "There was a man whose land was producing very well. He reasoned with himself, 'What should I do? I don't have enough storage space for all my crops.' Then he said, 'This is what I will do: I'll tear down my barns and build bigger ones, and I'll store all my grain and other goods there. Then I'll say to myself, "You're a blessed man! You have a huge supply of goods stored up that will last many years. Start taking it easy, eat, drink and have a great time!"' But God said to him, 'You fool! This very night you will die! And the things you stored up, who will own them?' That's how it is with anyone who stores up wealth for himself without being generous toward God."

Jesus said to his disciples, "For this reason, don't worry about your life and what you will eat or drink; or about your body and what you will wear. For life is more than food, and the body is more than clothing. Think about the ravens! They neither plant nor harvest, they don't have storerooms or barns, yet God feeds them. You are worth so much more than the birds! Can any of you by worrying extend his life by an hour? If you can't do a little thing like that, why worry about the rest? Think about the wild flowers, and how they grow. They neither work nor make yarn; yet, I tell you, not even Solomon in all his glory was clothed as beautifully as one of these. If this is how God clothes grass, which is alive in the field today and thrown in an oven tomorrow, how much more will he clothe you! What little trust you have!

"In other words, don't strive after what you will eat and drink, don't be anxious. For all the heathen nations in the world set their hearts on these things. Your Father knows that you need them too. Rather, seek his Kingdom and these things will be given to you as well. Don't worry, little flock, for your Father has chosen to give you the Kingdom! Sell what you own and do righteousness, make for yourselves purses that don't wear out, gathers riches in heaven that never fail, where no burglar comes near, where no moth destroys. For where your wealth(treasure) is, there your heart will be also.

"Be dressed and ready for action and have your lamps lit, like people waiting for their master's return after a wedding feast so that when he comes and knocks, they will open the door for him without delay. Happy are the servants whom the master finds alert when he comes! Yes! I'm telling you that he will put on his work clothes, seat them at the table, and come serve them himself! Whether it is late at night or early in the morning, if this is how he finds them, those servants are happy.

"But notice this: no home-owner would let his house be broken into if he knew when the thief was coming. You too, be ready! For the Son of Man will come when you are least expecting him."

Peter asked, "Lord, are you telling this parable for our benefit only or for everyone's?" He replied, "Now then, who is the trustworthy and sensible manager whose master puts him in charge of the household staff to give them their food at the proper time? It will go well with that servant if he is found doing his job when his master comes. Yes, I'm telling you he will put him in charge of all that he owns. But if that servant says to himself, 'My master is taking his time coming,' and starts mistreating the men and women servants, and eating and drinking, getting drunk. His master will come back on a day when the servant does not expect him, at a time he doesn't know in advance; his master will cut him in two and put him with the untrustworthy. Now the servant who knew what his master wanted but didn't prepare or act according to his will, will be whipped with many lashes; however, the one who did what deserves a beating, but didn't know, will not receive as many lashes. From him who has been given much, much will be demanded and from someone to whom people have entrusted much, they ask still more.

"I have come to set fire to the earth! And how I wish it were already kindled! I have a baptism to undergo, how pressured I feel until it is done! Do you think that I have come to bring peace in the Land? Not peace, but division! So, from now on a household of five will be divided, three against two, two against three.

Father will be against son, and son against father, mother against daughter and daughter against mother, mother-in-law against her daughter-in-law and daughter-in-law against mother-in-law." (Micah 7:6)

Then to the crowds Jesus said, "When you see dark clouds rising in the west, immediately you say that a rainstorm is coming; and when the wind is from the south, you say there will be a heat wave, and there is. Hypocrites! You know how to interpret the weather, how is it that you don't know how to interpret this present time? Why don't you see for yourselves what is right? If someone brings a lawsuit against you, be sure to settle with him first; otherwise he will take the matter to court, and the judge will turn you over to the bailiff, and the bailiff will throw you in jail. I tell you; you won't get out of there till you have paid the last penny!"

13

Forgiveness and repentance. Jesus heals on the Sabbath.

Just then, some people came to tell Jesus about the men from Galilee whom Pilate had murdered while they were preparing animals for sacrifice. His answer to them was, "Do you think that just because they died so horribly, these people from Galilee were worse sinners than all the others from Galilee? No, but unless you turn to God from your sins, you will all die just as they did!

"Or what about those eighteen people who died when the tower at Siloam fell on them? Do you think they were worse sinners than all the other people living in Jerusalem? No, I tell you. Rather, unless you turn from your sins, you will all die in a similar way."

Then Jesus gave this illustration: "A man had a fig tree planted in his vineyard, and he came looking for fruit on it but didn't find any. He said to the man who took care of the vineyard, 'Here, I've come looking for fruit on this fig tree for three years now without finding any. Cut it down, why keep wasting the soil?' The caretaker replied, 'Sir, leave it alone one more year. I'll dig around it and fertilize it. If it bears fruit next year, well and good; if not, you can then cut it down then.'"

Jesus was teaching in one of the synagogues on the Sabbath. A woman came up who had a spirit which had crippled her for eighteen years; she was bent, doubled over and unable to stand erect at all. On seeing her, Jesus called her and said to her, "Dear woman, you have been healed!" He laid his hands on her, and at once she stood upright and began to glorify God.

Now the president of the synagogue (local council), upset and angry that Jesus had healed on The Sabbath, spoke up and said to the congregation, "There are six days in the week for working; come during those days to be healed, not on The Sabbath!" However, the Lord addressed him, "You hypocrites! Don't each one of you untie your ox or your donkey from the stall and lead him off to drink on The Sabbath? This woman is a daughter of Abraham, and the Adversary kept her tied up for eighteen years! Shouldn't she be healed on The Sabbath?" By these words, Jesus put to shame the people who opposed him; but the rest of the crowd were happy about all the wonderful things that were taking place through him.

He went on to say, "What is the Kingdom of God like? What can we compare it with? It is like a mustard seed that a man planted in his garden, and it grew and became a tree, and the birds made nests in its branches."

And he also said, "With what will I compare the Kingdom of God? It is like yeast that a woman mixed in with a bushel of flour and waited until the whole batch of dough rose."

Jesus continued traveling through towns and villages, teaching and making his way toward Jerusalem. Someone asked him, "Are only a few people being saved?" He answered, "Struggle to get in through the narrow door, because I'm telling you that many will demand to get in and won't be able to enter once the owner of the house has gotten up and shut the door. You will stand outside, knocking at the door and saying, 'Lord! Open up for us!' But he will answer, 'I don't know you or where you come from!' Then you will say, 'We ate and drank with you! you taught in our streets!' and he will tell you, 'I don't know where you're from. Get away from me, all you workers of wickedness!' You will cry and grind your teeth when you see Abraham, Isaac, Jacob and all the prophets inside the Kingdom of God, but yourselves thrown out. More than that, people will come from the east, the west, the north and the south to sit at a table in the Kingdom of God. Notice that some who are last will be first, and some who are first will be last."

Just then, some Pharisees came up and said to Jesus, "Get out and get away from here, because Herod wants to kill you!" He said to them, "Go, tell that fox, 'Pay attention: today and tomorrow I am driving out demons and healing people, and on the third day I accomplish my goal.' Nevertheless, I must keep travelling today, tomorrow and the next day; because it is unthinkable that a prophet should die anywhere but in Jerusalem.

"Jerusalem! Jerusalem! You kill the prophets! You stone those who are sent to you! How often I wanted to gather your children, just as a hen gathers her chicks under her wings, but you refused! Look! God is abandoning your house to you! I tell you; you will not see me again until you say, 'Blessed is he who comes in the name of THE LORD!'" (Psalm 118:23)

Notes

14

Humility is greatness. The parable of what happens when people refuse the wealthy man's invitation.

One Sabbath when Jesus went to eat in the home of the leading Pharisees, there was a man in front of him whose body was swollen with fluid. Jesus spoke up and asked the Scriptures experts and Pharisees who were watching him closely, "Do the Scriptures allow healing on The Sabbath or not?" But they said nothing. So, putting his hands on him, he healed the man and sent him away. To them he said, "Which of you would not rescue a son or an ox that fell into a well on The Sabbath?" To these questions they could give no answer.

When Jesus noticed how the guests were choosing the best seats at the table, he told them this parable: "When you are invited by someone to a wedding feast, don't sit down in the best seat; because if there is someone more important than you who has been invited, the person who invited both of you might come and say to you and say 'this seat is reserved for the other man.' Then you will be humiliated as you go to take the least important place. Instead, go and sit in the least important place; so that when the one who invited you comes, he will say to you, 'Come on up, I have a better seat for you.' Then you will be honored in front of everyone sitting with you. Because everyone who exalts himself will be humbled, but everyone who humbles himself will be exalted."

Jesus also said to the one who had invited him, "When you host a dinner, don't invite your friends, brothers, relatives or rich neighbors; because they may well invite you in return, and that will be your repayment. Instead, when you have a party, invite poor people, disfigured people, the crippled, the blind! How blessed you will be that they have nothing with which to repay you! Because you will be repaid at the time of the resurrection."

When one of the people at the table heard this, he said to Jesus, "How blessed are those who eat bread in the Kingdom of God!" But he replied, "Once a man gave a banquet and invited many people. When the time came for the banquet, he sent his servant to tell those who had been invited, 'Come! Everything is ready!' But they responded with a chorus of excuses. The first said to him, 'I've just bought a field, and I have to go out and see it. Please accept my apologies.' Another said, 'I've just bought five yokes of oxen, and I'm on my way to test them out. Please accept my apologies.' Still another said, 'I just got married, so I can't come.' The servant reported these things to his master.

"Then the owner of the house, in a rage, told his servant, 'Quickly go out into the streets and side roads of the city; and bring in the poor, the disfigured, the blind and the crippled!' The servant said, 'Sir, we have done what you said, and there is still room.' The master said to the servant, 'Go out to the country roads and boundary walls, and insist people come in, so that my house will be full. I'm telling you that not one of those who were invited will get a taste of my banquet!'"

Large crowds were traveling along with Jesus. Turning, he said to them, "If anyone comes to me and does not hate (love less) his father, his mother, his wife, his children, his brothers and his sisters, yes, and even his own life, he cannot be my disciple. Whoever does not carry his own cross (deny himself) and come after me cannot be my disciple.

"Suppose one of you wants to build a tower. Don't you sit down and estimate the cost, to see if you have enough capital to complete it? If you don't, then when you have laid the foundation but can't finish, all the onlookers start making fun of you and say,

'This is the man who began to build, but was not able to finish!'

"Also, suppose one king is going out to wage a war with another king. Doesn't he first sit down and consider whether he, with his ten thousand troops, has enough strength to win than who is coming against him with twenty thousand? If he doesn't; then while the other is still far away, he sends a delegation to inquire about terms for peace.

"Understand that every one of you who doesn't renounce all that he has; cannot be my disciple. Salt is excellent. But if even the salt becomes tasteless, what can be used to season it? It is fit for neither soil nor fertilizer, so people throw it out. Whoever has ears that can hear, you must hear!"

Notes

LUKE; What He Said...

15

There is great joy in Heaven when one person repents.
The prodigal son.

The tax collectors and sinful people kept gathering around to hear Jesus, because of this, the Pharisees and Scripture-teachers kept grumbling. "This man," they said, "welcomes sinners and even eats with them!" So, Jesus told them this parable: "If one of you have a hundred sheep and lose one of them, don't you leave the other ninety-nine in the desert and look for the lost one until you find it? When he does find it, he joyfully hoists it onto his shoulders; and when he gets home, he calls his friends and neighbors together and says, 'Come, celebrate with me, because I have found my lost sheep!' I tell you that in the same way, there will be more joy in heaven over one sinner who turns to God from his sins than over ninety-nine righteous people who have no need to repent.

"Here is another example: what woman, if she has ten silver coins (engagement pledge)[1] and loses one of these valuable coins, wouldn't light a lamp, sweep the house and search everywhere until she finds it? And when she does find it, she calls her friends and neighbors together and says, 'Come, celebrate with me, because I have found the coin I lost.' In the same way, I tell you, there is joy among God's angels when one sinner repents."

Jesus also said, "A man had two sons. The younger of them said to him, 'Father, give me my share of our inheritance.'[2] So, the father divided the property between them. As soon as he could convert his share into cash, the younger son left home and went off to a distant country where he squandered his money in reckless living. But after he had spent it all, a severe famine arose throughout that country, and he began to experience hardship. So, he went and worked for one of the citizens of that country, who sent him into his fields to feed pigs.[3] He longed to fill his stomach with the carob pods[4] the pigs were eating, but no one gave him any.

"At last he came to his senses and said to himself, 'Any number of my father's hired workers have food to spare; and here I am, starving to death! I'm going to get up and go back to my father and say to him, "Father, I have sinned against Heaven and against you; I am no longer worthy to be called your son but would you treat me like one of your hired workers."' He got up and went back to his father.

"But while he was still a long way off, his father saw him and was moved with compassion. He ran and threw his arms around him and kissed him warmly. His son said to him, 'Father, I have sinned against Heaven and against you; I am no longer worthy to be called your son', but his father said to his servants, 'Quick, bring out a robe, the best one, and put it on him; and put a ring on his finger and shoes on his feet; and bring the fattened calf and kill it. Let's eat and have a celebration! For this son of mine was dead, but now he's alive again! He was lost, but now he has been found!' And they began celebrating.

"Now his older son was working in the field and as he came close to the house, he heard music and dancing. He called one of the servants and asked, 'What's going on?' The servant told him, 'Your brother has come back, and your father has slaughtered the calf that was fattened up, because he has gotten him back safe and sound.' But the older son became angry and refused to go inside.

"So, his father came out and pleaded with him. 'Look,' the son answered, 'I have worked for you all these years, and I have never disobeyed your orders. But you have never even given me a young goat, so that I could celebrate with my friends. Yet this son of yours comes, he squandered your property with prostitutes, and for him you slaughter the fattened calf!' 'Son, you are always with me,' said the father, 'and everything I have is yours. We had to celebrate and rejoice, because your brother was dead but has come back to life; he was lost but has now been found.'"

Notes

1. *The ten coins are presented to and accepted by the bride to be from the groom to be at the time of the engagement. These coins symbolized his ancestry and heritage. If she were to misplace one or more of these coins, it would be like saying she no longer wanted to marry him.*

2. *An inheritance was only distributed after the father of a family died. By asking for his inheritance, the son was indicating that he wished his father was dead. Deuteronomy 21: 18-21 states that a son that would do this should be stoned to death.*

3. *Pigs/swine were considered unclean and were never to be touched or tended to.*

4. *Carob pods were large seed pods which grew on trees. They were usually used for the feeding of livestock and horses. These were sometimes referred to as locusts. The seeds could be dries, ground up and used to make bread.*

16

You must not waste what He gives you. Story of the rich man who died.

Speaking to his disciples, Jesus said: "There was a wealthy man who employed a manager. Charges were brought to him that his manager was wasting his resources. In response, he summoned him and asked him, 'What is this I hear about you? Turn in your accounts, because you can no longer be manager.'

"'What am I to do?' the manager said to himself. 'My boss is firing me, I'm not strong enough to dig ditches, and I am too ashamed to go begging. Aha! I know what; I'll do something that will cause people will take me in after I've lost my job here!'

"So, after setting up meetings with each of his employer's debtors, he said to the first, 'How much do you owe my boss?' 'Eight hundred gallons of olive oil,' he replied. 'Take your (promissory)note back,' he told him. 'Now, quickly! Sit down and write one for four hundred!' To the next he said, 'And you, how much do you owe?' 'A thousand bushels of wheat,' he replied. 'Take your note back and write one for eight hundred.'

"And the employer of this corrupt manager commended him for acting so shrewdly! because the worldly have more nerve than those who have received the light in dealing with their own kind of people!

"Now what I say to you is this: use worldly wealth to make friends for yourselves, so that when it gives out, you may be welcomed into the eternal home. Someone who is trustworthy in a small matter is also trustworthy in large ones, and someone who is dishonest in a small matter is also dishonest in large ones. So, if you haven't been trustworthy in handling worldly wealth, who is going to trust you with the real thing? And if you haven't been trustworthy with what belongs to someone else, who will give you what should belong to you? No servant can be servant to two masters, for he will either hate the first and love the other or despise the second and be loyal to the first. You can't be a servant to both God and money."

The Pharisees heard all of this, and since they loved money, they ridiculed him. He said to them, "You people make yourselves look righteous to others, but God knows your hearts. What people regard highly is an abomination before God! Up to the time of John (the Baptist) there were the Scriptures and the Prophets. Since then the Good News of the Kingdom of God has been proclaimed, and everyone is pushing to get in. But it would be easier for heaven and earth to pass away than for one (brush)stroke of a letter in the Scriptures to become void. Every man who divorces his wife and marries another woman commits adultery, and a man who marries a woman divorced by her husband commits adultery. (Divorces for reasons other than unfaithfulness)

"Once there was a rich man who used to dress in the most expensive clothing and spent his days in magnificent luxury. At the gate of his home had been laid a beggar named Eleazar who was covered with sores. He would have been glad to eat the scraps that fell from the rich man's table; but instead. The dogs would come and lick his sores. In time the beggar died and was carried away by the angels to Abraham's side (the place where the righteous dead awaited judgement); the rich man also died and was buried.

"In Sheol (hell), where he was in torment, the rich man looked up and saw Abraham far away with Eleazar at his side. He called out, 'Father Abraham, take pity on me, and send Eleazar just to dip the tip of his finger in water to cool my tongue, because I'm in agony in this fire!' In reply Abraham said, 'Son, remember that when you were alive, you got the good things while he got the bad; but now he gets his consolation here, while you are the one in agony. Yet not only that: between you and us a deep rift has been established, so that those who would like to pass from here to you cannot, nor can anyone cross over from there to us.'

"He answered, 'Then, father, I beg you to send him to my father's house, where I have five brothers, to warn them; so that they may be spared having to come to this place of torment too.' But Abraham said, 'They have Moses and the Prophets; they should listen to them.' But, he said, 'No, father Abraham, they need more. If someone from the dead goes to them, they'll repent!' But he replied, 'If they won't listen to Moses and the Prophets, they won't be convinced even if someone rises from the dead!'"

Notes

17

Jesus warns anyone that misleads. He heals ten lepers and then speak of what it will be like after He is gone and then when he returns.

Jesus said to his disciples, "Without a doubt, traps will be set. Great suffering will be on the those who sets them! It would be better for him if he would have a millstone hung around his neck and thrown into the sea, rather than causing one of these little ones to go down the wrong path in life. Watch yourselves! If your brother sins against you, point it out to him; and then he repents, forgive him. Also, if seven times in one day he sins against you, and he repents you are to forgive him." The emissaries said to the Lord, "Increase our Faith (trust in God)." The Lord replied, "If you had trust as tiny as a mustard seed, you could say to this fig tree, 'Be uprooted and sent in the sea!' and it would obey you.

If one of you has a servant tending the sheep or plowing, when he comes back from the field, will you say to him, 'Come along now, sit down and eat'? No, you'll say, 'Get my dinner ready, dress up and serve me until I have finished eating and drinking; after that, you can eat and drink.' Does he thank the servant because he did what he was told to do? No! It's the same with you; when you have done everything you were told to do, you should be saying, 'We're just ordinary servants, we have only done our duty.'"

On his way to Jerusalem, Jesus passed along the border country between Samaria and the Galilee. As he entered one of the villages, ten men afflicted with leprosy met him. They stood at a distance and called out, "Jesus! Rabbi! Have compassion on us!"

On seeing them, he said, "Go have the priest examine you!" And as they went, they were healed. One of them, as soon as he realized he was healed, returned shouting praises to God, prostrating himself at Jesus' feet to thank him. This man was from Samaria. Jesus said, "Weren't ten people healed? Where are the other nine? What, no one else came back to give glory to God except this half-Jew?" To the man from Samaria he said, "Get up, you may go; your trust in God has saved you."

The Pharisees asked Jesus when the Kingdom of God would come. "The Kingdom of God," he replied, "does not come with visible signs; people will not be able to say, 'Look! Here it is!' or, 'Look over there!' Because the Kingdom of God is among you." Then he said to his disciples, "The time is coming when you will long to see even one of the days of the Son of Man (Jesus), but you will not see it. People will say to you, 'Look! Right here!' or, 'See! Over there!' Don't run off, don't follow them, because the Son of Man in his day will be like lightning that flashes and lights up the sky from one horizon to the other (speaking of His return). But first he must endure horrible suffering and be rejected by this generation.

"Also, at the time when the Son of Man returns, it will be just as it was at the time of Noah. People ate and drank, and men and women married, right up until the day Noah entered the ark; then the flood came and destroyed them all. Likewise, as it was in the time of Lot that people ate and drank, bought and sold, planted and built; but on the day Lot left Sodom, fire and sulfur rained down from heaven and destroyed them all. That is how it will be on the day the Son of Man is revealed. On that day, if someone is on the roof and his belongings are in his house, he must not go down to take them away. Similarly, if someone is in the field, he must not turn back to his old ways; remember Lot's wife! (turned to a pillar of salt) Whoever aims at preserving his own life will lose it, but whoever loses his life will live. Believe me, on that night there will be two people in one bed, one will be taken and the other left behind. There will be two women grinding grain together; one will be taken and the other left behind."

They asked him, "Where, Lord?" He answered, "Wherever there' is a dead body, that's where the vultures gather."

Notes

18

Then Jesus told his disciples another parable, in order to impress on them that they must always keep praying and trusting in your heart. "In a certain town, there was a judge who neither feared God nor respected other people. There was also in that town a widow who kept coming to him and saying, 'Give me a judgment against the man who is trying to ruin me.' For a long time he refused; but after a while, he said to himself, I'm not afraid of any man or God; but so I don't get worn out, I'll grant her request and she will stop bothering me!'"

Then Jesus said, "Notice what this corrupt judge said. Now won't God grant justice to his chosen people who cry out to him day and night? Is he delaying his answer? I tell you that he will judge in their favor, and quickly! But when the Son of Man comes, will he find this sort trust on the earth at all?"

Also, to those who thought they had everything figured out and looked down on everyone else, he told this parable: 'Two men went up to the Temple to pray, one a Pharisee and the other a tax-collector. The Pharisee stood and prayed to himself, 'O God! I thank you that I am not like the rest of the people; greedy, dishonest, immoral, or like this tax-collector! I fast twice a week, I pay tithes on all my income.' The tax-collector who was standing far off, would not even raise his eyes toward heaven, but beat his breast and said, 'God! Have mercy on me, I am a sinner!' I tell you; this man went home right with God rather than the other. Because everyone who exalts himself will be humbled, also everyone who humbles himself will be exalted."

People brought young children to Jesus so he would touch them; but when the disciples saw the people doing this, they rebuked them. However, Jesus called the children to him and said, "Let the children come to me, and stop hindering them, because the Kingdom of God belongs to such as these. Listen to me! whoever does not receive the Kingdom of God with a childlike attitude will not enter it at all!"

One of the leaders asked him, "Good rabbi, what should I do to obtain eternal life?" Jesus said to him, "Why are you calling me good? No one is good but God! You know the commandments; 'Don't commit adultery, don't murder, don't steal, don't give false testimony, honor your father and mother,'" (Deuteronomy 5:16-19) He replied, "I have kept all these since I was a boy." On hearing this Jesus said to him, "There is one thing you still lack. Sell whatever you have, distribute the proceeds to the poor, and you will have riches in heaven. Then come and follow me!" But when the man heard this, he became very sad, because he was very rich.

Jesus looked at him and said, "How hard it is for the rich to enter the Kingdom of God! It's easier for a camel to pass through a needle's eye than for a rich man to enter the Kingdom of God!" Those who heard this asked, "Then who can be saved?" He said, "What is impossible for man is possible with God."

Peter said, "Look, we have left our homes and followed you." Jesus said to them, "Yes! believe me that everyone who has left house, wife, brothers, parents or children, for the sake of the kingdom of God, will receive so much more in this time of history, and in the age to come; eternal life."

Then, taking the Twelve, Jesus said to them, "We are now going up to Jerusalem, where everything written through the prophets about the Son of Man will come true. He will be handed over to the Gentiles and be ridiculed, insulted and spat upon. Then, after they have beaten him, they will kill him. But on the third day he will rise from the dead." However, they didn't understand any of this; its meaning had been hidden from them, and they had no idea what he was talking about.

As Jesus approached Jericho, a blind man was sitting by the road, begging. When he heard the crowd going past, he asked what it was all about; and they told him, "Jesus from Nazareth is passing by." He called out, "Jesus! Son of David! (lineage of David). Have pity on me!" Those near the front scolded him in order to get him to shut up, but he shouted even louder, "Son of David! Have pity on me!" Jesus stopped and ordered the man to be brought to him. When he had come, Jesus asked him, "What do you want me to do for you?" The blind man said, "Lord, let me be able to see." Jesus said to him, "See again! your faith (in God) has healed you!" Instantly he received his sight and began following him, glorifying God; and when all the people saw it, they too praised God.

Notes

LUKE; What He Said...

19

Be faithful with a little and you will be trusted with more.
Jesus enters Jerusalem on a colt.

When Jesus was passing through Jericho a man named Zacchaeus; a wealthy Tax collector was trying to see who this Jesus was; he was short and could not see over the crowd. So, he ran on ahead and climbed a fig tree in order to see him, because Jesus was going to pass that way. When Jesus came to the place, he looked up and said to him, "Zacchaeus! Hurry! Come down, because I have to stay at your house!" He climbed down as fast as he could and welcomed Jesus joyfully. Everyone who saw it began muttering, "He has gone to be the guest of a sinner." Then Zacchaeus stood and said to him, "Here, Lord, I am giving half of all I own to the poor; and if I have cheated anyone, I will pay him back four times as much." Jesus said to him, "Today salvation has come to this house, for this man is also a son of Abraham. Because the Son of Man came to seek and save the lost."

While they were still gathered and listening to this, Jesus told a parable because he was near Jerusalem, and the people were thinking that the Kingdom of God was about to appear at any moment. "An important mam went to a country far away to have himself crowned king and then return. Calling ten of his servants, he gave them ten minas [about three months' wages] and said to them, 'Do business with this while I'm away.' But his fellow countrymen hated him, and they sent a delegation after the him to say, 'We don't want this man to rule over us.'

"However, when he returned, having been made king, he sent

for the servants to whom he had given the money, to find out what each one had earned in his business dealings. The first one came in and said, 'Sir, your minas has earned ten more coins.' 'Excellent!' he said to him. 'You are a good servant. Because you have been trustworthy in a small matter, I am putting you in charge of ten towns.' The second one came and said, 'Sir, your minas has earned five more coins; and to this one he said, 'You can oversee five towns.'

"Then another one came and said, 'Sir, here are your minas? I kept it hidden in a piece of cloth, because I was afraid of you because you take out what you didn't put in, and you harvest what you didn't plant.' To him the master said, 'You wicked servant! I will judge you by your own words! So, you knew, didn't you, that I was a severe man, taking out what I didn't put in and harvesting what I didn't plant? Then why didn't you put my money in the bank? Then, when I returned, I would have gotten it back with interest!' To those standing by, he said, 'Take the coin from him and give it to the one with ten coins.' They said to him, 'Sir, he already has ten coins!' But the master replied, 'I tell you, everyone who has something will be given more; but from anyone who has nothing, even what he does have will be taken away. However, as for these enemies of mine who did not want me to be their king, bring them here and execute them!'"

After saying this, Jesus went and began his way up to Jerusalem. As he approached Bethpage and Bethany, near the Mount of Olives, he sent two disciples, instructing them, "Go into the village ahead; on entering it, you will find a colt tied up that has never been ridden. Untie it and bring it here. If anyone asks why you are untying it, tell him, 'The Lord needs it.'" Those who were sent went off found it just as he had told them. As they were untying the colt, its owners said to them, "Why are you untying the colt?" and they said, "Because the Lord needs it." They brought it to Jesus; and, throwing their robes on the colt, they put Jesus on it. As he went along, people carpeted the road with their clothing; and as he came near Jerusalem, where the road descends from the

Mount of Olives, the entire gathering of disciples began to sing and praise God at the top of their voices for all the powerful works they had seen:

"Peace in Heaven!" and "Glory in the highest!" Some of the Pharisees in the crowd said to him, "Rabbi! Reprimand your disciples!" But he replied to them, "I tell you that if they keep quiet, the stones will shout out!" When Jesus had come closer and could see the city, he wept over it, saying, "If you only knew today what is needed for true peace! But now it is hidden from your sight. For the days are coming upon you when your enemies will set up a siege around you, encircle you, and box you in on every side, and throw you to the ground, you and your children within your walls, leaving not one stone standing on another; all because you did not recognize your opportunity when God offered it!"

Then Jesus entered the Temple grounds and began driving out those doing business there, saying to them, "The Scriptures say, 'My House is to be a house of prayer,' (Isaiah 56:7) but you have made it into a den of robbers!" (Jeremiah 7:11)

He taught at the Temple every day. The head priest, the Scripture-teachers and the leaders of the people tried to find a way to do away with him; but they couldn't find any way of doing it, because all the crowds were hanging onto his every word.

Notes

LUKE; What He Said...

20

Elders and teachers attempt to trick Jesus.

One day, as Jesus was teaching the people at the Temple, telling them about the Good News, the head priest and the Scriptures-teachers, along with the elders, came up to him and said, "Tell us, what authority do you have that allows you to do these things? Who gave you this authority?" He answered, "I will ask you a question as well. Tell me, the baptism of John, was it of Heaven or from men?" They discussed it among themselves, saying, "If we say, 'of Heaven,' he will say, 'Then why didn't you believe him?' But if we say, 'From men,' the crowds will stone us, because they're convinced that John was a prophet." So, they said, "We don't know where it came from." Jesus said to them, "Then I won't tell you by what authority I do these things."

Next Jesus told the people this parable: "A man planted a vineyard, rented it to tenant-farmers and went away for a long time. When the time came, he sent a servant to collect his share of the crop from the vineyard; but the tenants beat him up and sent him away empty-handed. He sent another servant and they beat him too, insulted him and sent him away empty-handed. He sent yet a third; this one they wounded and threw out.

"Then the owner of the vineyard said, 'What should I do? I'll send my son, whom I love; perhaps they will respect him.' But when the tenants saw him, they discussed it among themselves and said, 'This is the heir; let's kill him, so that the inheritance will be ours!' And they threw him out of the vineyard and killed him.

"Now what do you think the owner of the vineyard will do to

them? He will come and kill those tenants and give the vineyard to others!" When the people heard this, they said, "Heaven forbid!" But Jesus looked searchingly at them and said, "Then what is this scripture referring to?

'The very rock which the builders rejected has become the cornerstone'? (Psalm 118:22)

Whoever falls on that stone will be broken in pieces; but if it falls on him, he will be crushed to powder!"

The Scripture-teachers and the head priest would have grabbed him right then, because they knew that this parable was about them, but they were too afraid of the people.

They decided to keep a close eye on him. They sent spies who hypocritically represented themselves as righteous, so that they might find something Jesus said, as an excuse to hand him over to the authority of the governor. They put to him this religious question: "Rabbi, we know that you speak and teach straightforwardly, showing no partiality but really teaching what God's way is. Do the Scriptures permit us to pay taxes to the Roman Emperor or not?" But he, spotting their craftiness, said to them, "Show me a denarius! Whose name and picture does it have?" "The Emperor's," they replied. "Then," he said to them, "give the Emperor what belongs to the Emperor. And give God what belongs to God!" They were unable to use anything he said publicly to trap him; in fact, they were amazed at his answer and stayed silent.

Some Sadducees, who say there is no resurrection, came to Jesus and put to him a religious question: "Rabbi, Moses wrote for us that if a man dies leaving a wife but no children, his brother must take the wife and have children to preserve the man's family line.(Deuteronomy 25:5) Now there were seven brothers. The first took a wife and died childless, then the second and third took her, and likewise all seven, but they all died without leaving children. Lastly, the woman also died. In the Resurrection, which one's wife will she be? For all seven were married to her."

Jesus said to them, "In this present age, men and women marry; those judged worthy of the age to come, and of resurrection from the dead, do not get married, because they can no longer die. Being children of the Resurrection, they are like angels; but in fact, they are children of God.

"But even Moses showed that the dead are raised; for in the passage about the bush, he calls THE LORD 'the God of Abraham, the God of Isaac and the God of Jacob.' (Exodus 3:6:) Now he is not God of the dead, but of the living; to him all are alive."

Some of the Scripture-teachers answered, "Well spoken, Rabbi." For they no longer dared put to him a religious question. But he said to them, "How is it that people say the Messiah is David's son? For David himself says in the book of Psalms,

'THE LORD said to my Lord, "Sit at my right hand until I make your enemies your footstool."' (Psalm 11-:1)

David therefore calls him 'Lord.' So how can he be David's son?"

So that everyone could overhear, Jesus said to his disciples, "Watch out for the kind of Scripture-teachers that like to walk around in robes and be greeted with greater respect in the marketplaces, they like to have the best seats in the synagogues and the places of honor at banquets, the kind that take the houses belong to widows while making a show of formal prayers at great length. Their punishment will be so much the worse!"

Notes

21

Jesus predicts the destruction of the Temple. Says that that they will hear many terrible things but not be scared. There will be revelry and drinking but do not to be part of it because no one knows the hour of his return.

Then Jesus looked up, and as he watched the rich placing their gifts into the Temple[1] offering boxes, he also saw a poor widow put in two small coins. He said, "I tell you the truth, this poor widow has put in more than all the others. Because, out of their wealth, they gave money they could spare; but she, out of her poverty, has given all she had to live on."

As some people were remarking about the Temple, how beautiful its stonework and memorial decorations were, he said, "The time is coming when everything you see here will be totally destroyed, not a single stone will be left standing!" They asked him, "Rabbi, if this is so, when will these events take place? What sign will indicate to us that they are about to happen?" He answered, "Watch out! Don't be fooled! For many will come in my name, saying, 'I am he!' and, 'The time has come!' Don't go after them. When you hear of wars and revolts, don't panic. For these things must happen first, but the end will not happen immediately."

Then he told them, "Peoples will fight each other, nations will fight each other, there will be great earthquakes, there will be epidemics and famines in various places, and there will be terrifying sights and great signs from Heaven. But before all this happens, they will arrest you and persecute you, handing you over to the religious tribunals and prisons; and you will be brought before rulers and governors. This will all be on account of me, but it will prove an opportunity for you to bear witness. So, make up your minds not to worry, rehearsing your defense beforehand; for I myself will give you an eloquence and a wisdom that no adversary will be able to resist or refute. You will be betrayed even by parents, brothers, relatives and friends; they will put some of you put to death; and many will hate you because of me. But not a hair of your head will be lost. By standing firm you will save your lives. "However, when you see Jerusalem surrounded by armies, then you are to understand that she is about to be destroyed.

Those in Judea must escape to the hills, those inside the city must get out, and those out in the country must stay away. For these are the days of vengeance, when everything that has been written in the Scriptures will come true. What a terrible time it will be for pregnant women and nursing mothers! For there will be great distress in the Land and judgment on the people. Some will die by weapons, others will be taken into the many countries of the Gentiles, and Jerusalem will be trampled down by the Gentiles until the time of the unbelievers has run its course.

"There will appear signs in the sun, moon and stars; and on the earth, nations will be worried and mystified at the sound and surge of the sea, as people faint with the thought of what is overtaking the world; for the powers in heaven will be shaken. (Haggai 2:21) Then they will see the Son of Man coming in a cloud (Daniel 7:13) with tremendous power and glory. When these things start to happen, stand up and hold your heads high; because you are about to be redeemed!"

Jesus proceeded to tell them an allegory: "Consider the fig trees, actually, all the trees. As soon as they sprout leaves, you can see for yourselves that summer is near. In the same way, when you see these things taking place, you are to know that the Kingdom of God is near! Yes! I tell you that this generation will certainly not pass away before it has all happened. Heaven and earth will pass away, but my words will certainly not pass away.

"Be careful, or your hearts will become dulled by revelry, drunkenness and the worries of everyday living, and that Day will be sprung upon you suddenly like a trap! For it will close in on everyone no matter where they live throughout the whole world. Stay alert, always praying that you will have the strength to escape all the things that will happen and to stand in the presence of the Son of Man."

Jesus spent his days at the Temple, teaching; while at night he went out and stayed on the hill called the Mount of Olives. All the people would get up in the morning to come and hear him at the Temple courts.

Notes

1   *The temple was the pace where offerings were brought and sacrifices were made to atone for sins.*

LUKE; What He Said...

22

The festival of unleavened bread, known as Passover,[1] was approaching; and the head priest and the Scripture-teachers began trying to find some way to get rid of Jesus, because they were afraid of the people.

At this point the Adversary went into Judas who was from Iscariot, one of the Twelve. He approached the head priest and the Temple guard and discussed with them how he might turn Jesus over to them. They were pleased with this and offered to pay him money. He agreed and began looking for the opportunity to betray Jesus without anyone knowing.

When the day of unleavened bread had arrived, the Passover lamb had to be sacrificed. Jesus sent Peter and John, instructing them, "Go and prepare our Feast, so we can eat." They asked him, "Where do you want us to prepare it?" He told them, "As you go into the city, a man carrying a jar of water will meet you. Follow him into the house he enters, and say to its owner, 'The Rabbi asks you, "Where is the guest room, where I am to eat the Passover meal with my disciples?"' He will show you a large room upstairs already furnished; get everything ready there." They went and found everything just as Jesus had told them they would be, then prepared for the Feast.

When the time came, Jesus and the emissaries (the twelve) reclined at the table, and he said to them, "I have really wanted to celebrate this Feast with you before I die! It is certain that I will not celebrate it again until it is given its full meaning in the Kingdom of God."

Then, taking a cup of wine, he made the blessing and said, "Take this and share it among yourselves. I'm telling you that from now on, I will not drink the 'fruit of the vine' until the Kingdom of God comes." Also, taking a piece of unleavened bread, he made the blessing, broke it, gave it to them and said, "This is my body, which is being given for you; do this in memory of me." He did the same with the cup after the meal, saying, "This cup is the New Covenant, ratified by my blood, which is being poured out for you.

"Look! The person who is betraying me is here at the table with me! The Son of Man is going to his death according to God's plan, but what bitter suffering for the man who is betraying him!" They began asking each other which of them could do such a thing.

An argument arose among them as to which of them should be considered the greatest. But Jesus said to them, "The kings of the Gentiles lord it over them; and those in authority over them are given the title, 'Benefactor.' But not so with you! On the contrary, let the greater among you become like the younger, and the one who in charge becomes like one who serves. For who is greater? The one reclining at the table? or the one who serves? It's the one reclining at the table, isn't it? But I myself am among you like one who serves.

"You are the ones who have stayed with me throughout my trials. Just as my Father gave me the right to rule, so I give you an appointment, specifically to eat and drink at my table in my Kingdom and to sit on thrones judging the twelve tribes of Israel.

"Simon, Simon, listen to me! The Adversary demanded to have you for himself, to sift you like wheat! But I prayed for you, Simon, that your trust might not fail. And you, when you have repented, strengthen your brothers!" Simon said to him, "Lord, I am prepared to go with you both to prison and to die!" Jesus replied, "Peter, the rooster will not crow today until you have denied three times that you know me."

He said to them, "When I sent you out without wallet, pack or shoes, were you ever short of anything?" "Not a thing," they answered. "But now," he said, if you have a wallet or a pack, take it; and if you don't have a sword, sell your robe to buy one. For I tell you this: the passage from the Scriptures that says, 'He was counted with transgressors,' (Isaiah 53:12) has to be fulfilled in me; since what is happening to me has a purpose." They said, "Look, Lord, there are two swords right here!" "Enough!" he replied.

When he left, Jesus went as usual to the Mount of Olives; and the disciples followed him. When he arrived, he said to them, "Pray that you won't be put to the test." He went about a stone's throw away from them, kneeled and prayed, "Father, if you are willing, take this cup away from me; nevertheless, let not my will but yours be done." There appeared to him an angel from heaven giving him strength, and in great anguish he prayed more intensely, so that his sweat became like drops of blood falling to the ground. On getting up from prayer and coming to the disciples, he found them sleeping because of their grief. He said to them, "Why are you sleeping? Get up and pray that you won't be put to the test!"

While he was still speaking, a crowd of people arrived, with the man called Judas (one of the Twelve!) leading them. He came up to Jesus to kiss him, but Jesus said to him, "Judas, are you betraying the Son of Man with a kiss?" When his followers saw what was going to happen, they said, "Lord, should we use our swords?" One of them struck out at the servant of the high priest and cut off his right ear. But Jesus said, "Just let me do this," and, touching the man's ear, he healed him.

Then Jesus said to the head priest, the officers of the Temple guard and the elders who had come to seize him, "So you came out just as you would to the leader of a rebellion, with swords and clubs? Every day I was there with you in the Temple court, yet you didn't arrest me. But this is your hour; the hour when darkness rules."

After seizing him, they led him away and brought him into the house of the high priest. Peter followed at a distance; but when they had lit a fire in the middle of the courtyard and sat down together, Peter joined them. One of the servant girls saw him sitting in the light of the fire, stared at him and said, "This man also was with him." But he denied it: "Lady, I don't even know him." A little later, someone else saw him and said, "You're one of them too"; but Peter said, "Man, I am not!" About an hour later, another man asserted emphatically, "There can be no doubt that this fellow was with him, because he too is from Galilee!" But Peter said, "I don't know what you're talking about!" right then, while he was still speaking, a rooster crowed. The Lord turned and looked straight at Peter. Then Peter remembered what the Lord had told him, "Before the rooster crows today, you will deny me three times." So, he went outside and cried bitterly.

Meanwhile, the men who were holding Jesus made fun of him. They beat him, blindfolded him, and kept asking him, "'prophesy'! Who hit you that time?" And they said many other insulting things to him.

At daybreak, the people's council of elders, including both head priest and Scriptures-teachers, met and led him off to their Sanhedrin (religious court), where they said, "If you are the Messiah, tell us." He answered, "If I tell you, you won't believe me; and if I ask you, you won't answer. But from now on, the Son of Man will be sitting at the right hand of The Almighty," (Psalm 100:1) Then they said, "Does this mean, then, that you are the Son of God?" And he replied, "You say I am." They said, "Why do we need additional testimony? We have heard it ourselves from his own mouth!"

Notes

1   *Passover was one of the three major holy days in Israel. This commemorates the night in Egypt when the angel of death visited to kill the firstborn child of every household. The Israelites sacrifice lambs without any blemish and put is blood of the lintel and door post of their home. This was the sign that the angel of death could not enter and kill.*

23

Jesus is sentenced to death and is crucified.
A criminal asks him for forgiveness.

Then, the whole Sanhedrin adjourned and brought Jesus before Pilate, where they accused him. "We found this man undermining our nation, forbidding us to pay taxes to Caesar and claiming that he himself is the Messiah; a king!" Pilate then asked him, "Are you the king of the Jews?" Jesus replied, "The words are yours." Pilate said to the head priest and the crowds, "I don't see any basis for a charge to be against this man." But they persisted. "He is stirring up the people with his teaching all around Judea. He began in Galilee, them came here!" When Pilate heard this, he asked if the man was from the Galilee and learned that he was under Herod's jurisdiction, he sent him over to Herod, who at that time happened to be in Jerusalem.

Herod was happy to see Jesus, because he had heard about him and for a long time had been wanting to meet him; in fact, he hoped to see him perform a miracle. He questioned him at great length, but Jesus would not answer. However, the head priest and the Scripture-teachers stood there, vehemently accusing him. Herod and his soldiers treated Jesus with contempt and made fun of him. Then, dressing him in an expensive robe, they sent him back to Pilate. That day Herod and Pilate became friends with each other; previously they had been enemies.

Pilate summoned the head priest, the leaders and the people, and said to them, "You brought this man before me on a charge of undermining the people. I examined him in your presence and did not find the man guilty of the crime you are accusing him of. Neither did Herod, because he sent him back to us. It is obvious that he has not done anything that he deserves to be executed. So, I'm going to have him flogged, then release him." But they shouted, "Away with this man! Give us Barabbas!"[1] Then Pilate appealed to them again, because he wanted to release Jesus. They shouted even louder, "Crucify him! Execute him" A third time he asked them, "But what did he do wrong? I see no reason to put him to death. Therefore, I'm going to have him flogged and set free." But they went on yelling insistently, demanding that he be executed on the a cross; and their shouting prevailed. Pilate decided to grant their demand. He released the man who had been thrown in prison for insurrection and murder, the one they had asked for and Jesus gave into their will.

As the Roman soldiers led Jesus away, they grabbed hold of a man from Cyrene named Simon, who was on his way in from the country. They put part of the execution cross on his back and made him carry it behind Jesus. Many people followed, including women crying and wailing for him. Jesus turned to them and said, "Daughters of Jerusalem, stop weeping for me; but instead weep for yourselves and your children! For the time is coming when people will say, 'The women without children are the fortunate ones; those whose wombs have never conceived and birthed a child, whose breasts have never nursed a baby!

Then they will begin to say to the mountains, 'Fall on us!' and to the hills, 'Cover us!' (Hosea 10:8)

For if they do these things when the tree is green, what is going to happen when it's dry?"

Two other men, both criminals, were led out to be executed with him. When they came to the place called The Skull, they nailed him to a cross; and they nailed the criminals to crosses, one on the right and one on the left. Jesus said, "Father, forgive them; they don't know what they are doing."

Gambling, the soldiers divided up his clothes by throwing dice. (Psalm 22:18) The crowd stood watching, and the rulers sneered at him. (Psalm 22:7) "He saved others," they said, "so if he really is the Messiah, the one chosen by God, let him save himself!" The soldiers scoffed at him; and offered him vinegar and said, "If you are the king of the Jews, save yourself!" And there was a sign over him which read,

THIS IS THE KING OF THE JEWS

One of the criminals that was hanging there, shouted insults at him. "Aren't you the Messiah? Save yourself and us too!" But the other one spoke up and admonished the first, saying, "Don't you fear God? You're getting the same punishment as he is. Ours is only fair; we're getting what we deserve for what we did. But this man did nothing wrong." Then he said, "Jesus, remember me when you return as King." Jesus said to him, "Yes! I promise that you will be with me today in Paradise."

Beginning around noon, darkness covered the entire Land until three o'clock in the afternoon; there was no sun. Also, the veil in the Temple was ripped down the middle. Crying out with a loud voice, Jesus said, "Father! Into your hands I commit my spirit." (Psalm 31:5) With these words he gave up his spirit.

When the Roman officer saw what had happened, he began to praise God and said, "Surely this man was innocent!" When everyone that had gathered to watch the execution saw the things that had occurred, they returned home in terrible sorrow. All his friends, including the women who came him from the Galilee with him, had been standing at a distance and witnessed everything that day.

There was a good man named Joseph, a member of the Sanhedrin(council). He was a righteous person; and he had not agreed with either the Sanhedrin's motivations or actions. He was from the town of Arimathea, a town in Judea and he was looking forward to the Kingdom of God. He approached Pilate and asked for Jesus' body. He was granted permission and he took it down, wrapped it in a linen sheet, and placed it in a new tomb which had been cut into some rock.

It was Friday which was preparation Day, and a Sabbath was about to begin. The women who had come with Jesus from Galilee followed; they saw the tomb and how his body was placed in it. Then they went back home to prepare spices and ointments.

On the Sabbath the women rested, in obedience to the commandment.

Notes

1. *Barabbas was a man who had been thrown in prison for inciting a riot and for murder.*

24

Jesus is raised from the dead and appears to his followers.

On the next day, while it was early, they took the spices and ointments that they had prepared and went to the tomb. They found the stone rolled away from the tomb! When they entered it, they discovered that the body of the Lord Jesus was gone! While they were standing there wondering about it, two men in dazzlingly bright clothing stood next to them. Terror-stricken, they bowed down with their faces to the ground. The two men said to them, "Why are you looking for the living among the dead? He is not here; he has been raised from the dead. Remember what he told you while he was still in the Galilee, 'The Son of Man must be delivered into the hands of sinful men and be executed on a wooden cross as a criminal, but on the third day he would be raised again'?" Then they remembered his words and hurried back from the tomb, then told everything to the Eleven and to the rest gathered there. The women who told the emissaries these things were Mary of Magdala, Joanna, Mary the mother of James, and several others with them.

But the disciples didn't believe them; in fact, they thought that what they said was ridiculous! However, Peter got up and ran to the tomb. Stooping down, he saw only the burial cloths and went home wondering what had happened.

That same day, two of Jesus' disciples were going to a village about seven miles from Jerusalem called Emmaus, and they were talking with each other about all the things that had happened. As they talked and discussed it, Jesus himself came up and walked along with them, but something prevented them from recognizing him.   He asked them, "What are you talking about with each other?" They stopped walking sadly along; One of them, named Cleopas, replied to him, "Are you the only one staying in Jerusalem that doesn't know the things that have been going on there the last few days?" "What things?" he asked them. They said to him, "The things about Jesus from Nazareth. He was a prophet and demonstrated it by the miracles he did and said before God and all the people. Our head priest and our leaders handed him over, to be sentenced to death and executed on a cross as a criminal. We had hoped that he would be the one to liberate Israel. Today is the third day since these things happened; and this morning, some of the women had an amazing report. They were at the tomb early and couldn't find his body, so they came back. They told us that they had seen a vision of angels who say Jesus is alive! Some of our friends went to the tomb and found it just as the women had said."

He said to them, "Foolish people! Why is it so hard for you to not trust what the prophets wrote in the Scriptures? Didn't the Messiah have to die like this before entering his glory?" Then, starting with Moses and the prophets, he explained to them the things that can be found throughout the Scriptures concerning himself.

As they neared the village, He acted as if he were going on further; but stalling him they requested "Stay with us, for it's almost evening and it's getting dark." So, he went in to stay with them. As he sat with them at the table, he took the unleavened bread, made the blessing, broke it and handed it to them. Then their eyes were opened, and they recognized him. But then he disappeared. They said to each other, "Didn't our hearts burn inside us as he spoke to us on the road, explaining the Scriptures to us?"

Right away they returned to Jerusalem and found the Eleven gathered together with their friends, saying, "It's true! The Lord has risen! Simon Peter saw him!" Then the two told the story of happened on the road and how he recognized him when breaking the unleavened bread.

They were still talking about it when there he was, standing among them! Startled and terrified, they thought they were seeing a ghost. But he said to them, "Why are you so upset? Why are doubts welling up inside you? Look at my hands and my feet, it is really me! Touch me and see, a spirit doesn't have a real body, you can see that I do." as he showed them his hands and feet. While they were still unable to believe it for joy and stood there dumbfounded, he said to them, "Have you have anything I can eat?" They gave him a piece of broiled fish, which he took and ate in their presence.

Jesus said to them, "This is what I meant when I was still with you and told you that everything written about me in the Scriptures of Moses, the Prophets and the Psalms had to be fulfilled." Then he opened their minds, so that they could understand the Scriptures, telling them, "Here is what it says: the Messiah is to suffer and to rise from the dead on the third day; and in his name repentance leading to forgiveness of sins is to be proclaimed to people from all nations, starting with Jerusalem. You are witnesses of these things. Now I am sending forth upon you what my Father promised, so stay here in the city until you have been equipped with power from above."

He led them out toward Bethany; then, raising his hands, he said a blessing over them; and as he was blessing them, he withdrew from them and was brought up into heaven. They bowed in worship to him, then returned to Jerusalem, overflowing with joy. And they spent all their time in the Temple courts, praising God.

LUKE; What He Said...

Notes

Authors thoughts.

If this book has inspired you, please let people know. If you would like more information regarding the Christian Faith, please visit your local church. Pastors would love to share their faith and stories with you.

If you have arrived at the point in which you would like to become a Christian and give your future to God, simply say the following prayer out loud from the depths of your being.

"Father, God, I believe that you sent your Son to die for me, to save me from my sins. I choose right now to accept Jesus the Christ as my Lord and Savior and will follow you with all I am."

If you said this prayer, CONGRATULATIONS, you name is now in the Book of Life!

Please get involved in the Christian community and grow in your faith.

LUKE; What He Said...